Better Homes and Gardens®

Bigger Better Burgers

Our seal assures you that every recipe in *Bigger Better Burgers*
has been tested in the Better Homes and Gardens® Test Kitchen.
This means that each recipe is practical and reliable,
and meets our high standards of taste appeal.

BETTER HOMES AND GARDENS. BOOKS

Editor: Gerald M. Knox
Art Director: Ernest Shelton
Managing Editor: David A. Kirchner
Copy and Production Editors: James D. Blume, Marsha Jahns,
    Rosanne Weber Mattson, Mary Helen Schiltz

Food and Nutrition Editor: Nancy Byal
Department Head, Cook Books: Sharyl Heiken
Associate Department Heads: Sandra Granseth,
    Rosemary C. Hutchinson, Elizabeth Woolever
Senior Food Editors: Julia Malloy, Marcia Stanley,
    Joyce Trollope
Associate Food Editors: Barbara Atkins, Linda Foley, Linda Henry,
Lynn Hoppe, Mary Jo Plutt, Maureen Powers, Martha Schiel
Recipe Development Editor: Marion Viall
Test Kitchen Director: Sharon Stilwell
Test Kitchen Photo Studio Director: Janet Pittman
Test Kitchen Home Economists: Jean Brekke, Kay Cargill,
    Marilyn Cornelius, Jennifer Darling, Maryellyn Krantz,
    Lynelle Munn, Dianna Nolin, Marge Steenson,
    Cynthia Volcko

Associate Art Directors: Linda Ford Vermie, Neoma Alt West,
    Randall Yontz
Assistant Art Directors: Lynda Haupert, Harijs Priekulis,
    Tom Wegner
Senior Graphic Designers: Jack Murphy, Stan Sams,
    Darla Whipple-Frain
Graphic Designers: Mike Burns, Sally Cooper, Blake Welch,
    Brian Wignall, Kimberly Zarley
Vice President, Editorial Director: Doris Eby
Executive Director, Editorial Services: Duane L. Gregg

Senior Vice President, General Manager: Fred Stines
Director of Publishing: Robert B. Nelson
Vice President, Retail Marketing: Jamie Martin
Vice President, Direct Marketing: Arthur Heydendael

BIGGER BETTER BURGERS

Editor: Linda Henry
Copy and Production Editor: Marsha Jahns
Graphic Designer: Darla Whipple-Frain
Electronic Text Processor: Donna Russell
Contributing Photographers: Mike Dieter, M. Jensen
    Photography, Inc., Sid Spelts Photography
Food Stylists: Janet Pittman, Maria Rolandelli
Contributing Illustrator: Thomas Rosborough

On the cover: Put together a burger creation of your own, as
we did here, by choosing meat mixtures, condiments, and buns from
the many delicious possibilities in this book.

Contents

Two-Fisted Burgers

1 tablespoon lemon juice
1½ teaspoons Worcester-
    shire sauce
⅛ teaspoon garlic powder
1½ pounds lean ground beef
4 slices American *or*
    cheddar cheese

● In a medium mixing bowl combine lemon juice, Worcestershire sauce, and garlic powder. Add ground beef and mix well. Shape meat mixture into eight ¼-inch-thick patties.

    Place patties on an unheated rack in a broiler pan. Broil 3 to 4 inches from the heat about 4 minutes total or till done, turning once. *Or,* grill patties, on an uncovered grill, directly over *medium-hot* coals for 5 to 7 minutes total or till done, turning once. Top *4* cooked patties with cheese. Heat just till cheese melts.

Check the bakery for unsplit kaiser rolls. But in a jam, buy split ones and cut a thin layer off the top or bottom half so you end up with three slices.

4 unsplit kaiser rolls
    Mustard *or* catsup
4 lettuce leaves
4 onion slices
4 tomato slices
    Sweet pickle relish
    or dill pickle slices
¼ cup Thousand Island salad
    dressing

● To serve, split rolls lengthwise into thirds. Spread mustard or catsup on bottom slice of each roll. Layer the roll with lettuce, an onion slice, a cooked patty without cheese, the middle slice of a kaiser roll, a tomato slice, a cooked patty with melted cheese, and pickle relish or slices. Spread a little salad dressing on the top slice of each roll and place it atop relish or pickles. Makes 4 servings.

Coney Burgers

1 beaten egg
1 10-ounce can tomatoes and green chili peppers
2 tablespoons fine dry bread crumbs
½ teaspoon chili powder
1 pound lean ground beef
2 frankfurters

● In a medium mixing bowl combine egg, ¼ *cup* of the tomatoes and green chili peppers, bread crumbs, and chili powder. Add ground beef and mix well.

Cut frankfurters in half lengthwise. Shape ¼ of the meat mixture around *each* frankfurter half.

Place meat-wrapped frankfurters on an unheated rack in a broiler pan. Broil 4 to 5 inches from the heat for 8 to 10 minutes total or till done, turning once.

---

1 teaspoon cornstarch
1 teaspoon chili powder
1 8-ounce can red kidney beans, drained

● Meanwhile, in a small saucepan combine the remaining tomatoes and green chili peppers, cornstarch, and chili powder. Cook and stir till thickened and bubbly, then cook and stir for 2 minutes more. Stir in beans and heat through.

---

4 frankfurter buns, split and toasted
Shredded cheddar cheese

● Serve meat-wrapped frankfurters in buns with bean mixture. Sprinkle with cheddar cheese. Makes 4 servings.

Mmm, mmm, mmm. There's nothing better than juicy burgers on crispy, toasted buns. To toast your frankfurter or hamburger buns, place them, cut side up, on the broiler rack around the burgers. Broil for 1 to 2 minutes, watching closely so the buns don't get too dark.

Frank Facts

Bet your guests two bits that they don't know all these frank facts!

● The guy who put the bun around the wiener came from St. Louis. A sausage vendor at the 1904 World's Fair furnished his customers with white gloves to make eating the hot wieners easier. Customers were to return the gloves, but most didn't. So, the vendor's brother-in-law, a baker, thought of placing the sausages in long, slender buns.

● Because dachshunds and franks are similar in shape, folks labeled them "dachshund sausages." An artist created talking sausage-shaped cartoon characters but finding dachshund hard to spell and even harder to say, he nicknamed his characters "hot dogs." Since then, the cartoon has disappeared but the name lives on.

Avocado Salsa Burgers

Avocado Salsa
1 beaten egg
¼ cup sour cream dip with French onion
¼ cup fine dry bread crumbs
¼ teaspoon salt
Dash pepper
1 pound lean ground beef

● Prepare the Avocado Salsa.

In a medium mixing bowl combine egg and sour cream dip. Stir in bread crumbs, salt, and pepper. Add ground beef and mix well. Shape meat mixture into 4 oval patties, each about 5 inches long and ½ inch thick.

Place patties on an unheated rack in a broiler pan. Broil 3 to 4 inches from the heat to desired doneness, turning once (allow about 9 minutes total for medium). *Or,* grill patties, on an uncovered grill, directly over *medium-hot* coals to desired doneness, turning once (allow 6 to 8 minutes total for medium).

2 large pita bread rounds, halved crosswise

● Serve burgers in pita halves with some Avocado Salsa. Pass remaining salsa. Makes 4 servings.

Avocado Salsa: Stir together 1 medium *avocado,* peeled, seeded, and chopped; 1 small *tomato,* seeded and chopped; 2 slices crisp-cooked *bacon,* crumbled; 2 tablespoons finely chopped *onion;* 1 tablespoon diced *canned green chili peppers;* 1 tablespoon *lemon juice;* and ⅛ teaspoon *salt.* Cover and chill about 2 hours. Makes about 2 cups.

A lot of pinching, poking, tapping, and sniffing goes on in the produce section of a supermarket—all in search of the perfectly ripened fruit or vegetable. So what test works best for a ripe avocado?

Cradle the avocado in the the palm of your hand. If it yields to gentle pressure, it's ready to use (and you can store it in the refrigerator for up to three days). If there's some firmness, store the avocado at room temperature till it reaches the right softness.

To make sure the avocado is at just the right stage of ripeness, play it safe and shop for one a few days ahead.

Burgers with Curried Zucchini Relish

Curried Zucchini Relish (see recipe, right)	● Prepare Curried Zucchini Relish.	**Curried Zucchini Relish:** In a medium saucepan combine 1 small *zucchini*, chopped (1 cup); 1 medium *tomato*, chopped (¾ cup); ¼ cup chopped *onion*; ¼ cup chopped *green pepper*; 1 teaspoon *brown sugar*; 1 teaspoon *curry powder*; ¼ teaspoon *salt*; 1 small clove *garlic*, minced; dash *pepper*; and 1 *bay leaf*. Cook and stir till liquid starts to form. Reduce the heat and simmer, covered, for 10 minutes, stirring occasionally. Remove the bay leaf. Cool slightly.
1 beaten egg ¼ cup dairy sour cream ⅓ cup fine dry bread crumbs ¼ cup chopped peanuts ¼ teaspoon salt ¼ teaspoon ground cinnamon Dash pepper 1½ pounds lean ground beef	● In a medium mixing bowl combine egg and sour cream. Stir in bread crumbs, peanuts, salt, cinnamon, and pepper. Add ground beef and mix well. Shape mixture into 6 oval patties, each about 5 inches long and ½ inch thick. Place patties on an unheated rack in a broiler pan. Broil 3 to 4 inches from the heat to desired doneness, turning once (allow about 9 minutes total for medium). *Or,* grill patties, on an uncovered grill, directly over *medium-hot* coals to desired doneness, turning once (allow 6 to 8 minutes total for medium).	Place *half* of the relish mixture in a blender container or food processor bowl. Cover and blend or process till smooth. Stir in remaining relish mixture. Cover and chill. Makes about 1 cup.
3 large pita bread rounds, halved crosswise	● Serve burgers in pita halves with some Curried Zucchini Relish. Pass remaining relish. Makes 6 servings.	

Tangy Beer Burgers

1 beaten egg ⅓ cup beer ⅓ cup fine dry bread crumbs ¼ cup finely chopped onion 2 tablespoons grated Parmesan cheese 1½ pounds lean ground beef Tangy Beer Sauce (see recipe, right)	● In a medium mixing bowl combine egg and beer. Stir in bread crumbs, onion, and Parmesan cheese. Add ground beef and mix well. Shape meat mixture into six ¾-inch-thick patties. Place patties on an unheated rack in a broiler pan. Broil 3 to 4 inches from heat to desired doneness, turning once (allow about 12 minutes total for medium). *Or,* grill patties, on an uncovered grill, directly over *medium-hot* coals to desired doneness, turning once (allow 10 to 12 minutes total for medium). Brush burgers occasionally with Tangy Beer Sauce after turning.	**Tangy Beer Sauce:** In a small saucepan combine ⅓ cup *chili sauce*, ¼ cup *beer*, 2 teaspoons *prepared horseradish*, 1 teaspoon *cornstarch*, ¼ teaspoon *dry mustard*, and ⅛ teaspoon *pepper*. Cook and stir till thickened and bubbly, then cook and stir for 2 minutes more. Makes ¾ cup.
6 lettuce leaves 6 hamburger buns, split and toasted	● Serve burgers on lettuce-lined buns. Pass remaining sauce. Makes 6 servings.	

Round burgers don't fit inside taco shells very well, so we made these burgers oval instead.

Pat the ground beef mixture into oval patties, making each patty about 5 inches long and ½ inch thick.

Taco Burgers

1 beaten egg
2 tablespoons catsup
¼ cup fine dry bread crumbs
1 to 1½ teaspoons chili powder
1 teaspoon Worcestershire sauce
½ teaspoon garlic salt
¼ teaspoon dry mustard
1 pound lean ground beef

● In a medium mixing bowl combine egg and catsup. Stir in bread crumbs, chili powder, Worcestershire sauce, garlic salt, and mustard. Add ground beef and mix well. Shape the ground beef mixture into 8 oval patties, each about 5 inches long and ½ inch thick.

Place patties on an unheated rack in a broiler pan. Broil 3 to 4 inches from the heat to desired doneness, turning once (allow about 9 minutes total for medium). *Or,* grill patties, on an uncovered grill, directly over *medium-hot* coals to desired doneness, turning once (allow 6 to 8 minutes total for medium).

8 taco shells
Shredded lettuce
Shredded cheddar *or* American cheese
Chopped tomato

● Serve burgers in taco shells with lettuce, cheese, and chopped tomato. Makes 4 servings.

Besides lettuce, cheese, and tomato, try topping your Taco Burgers with some sliced ripe olives, a dollop of sour cream, and taco sauce or salsa.

Java Burgers

⅓ cup catsup
¼ cup water
2 tablespoons chopped onion
1 teaspoon instant coffee crystals
½ teaspoon Worcestershire sauce
1 small clove garlic, minced

● For barbecue sauce, combine catsup, water, onion, coffee crystals, Worcestershire sauce, garlic, and dash *pepper*. Simmer, uncovered, for 10 to 15 minutes or till desired consistency.

1 beaten egg
¼ cup fine dry bread crumbs
1 pound lean ground beef
4 hamburger buns, split and toasted

● Combine egg and *2 tablespoons* barbecue sauce. Stir in bread crumbs. Add ground beef and mix well. Shape mixture into four ¾-inch-thick patties.
Place patties on an unheated rack in a broiler pan. Broil 3 to 4 inches from heat to desired doneness, turning once (allow about 12 minutes total for medium). *Or,* grill patties, on an uncovered grill, directly over *medium-hot* coals to desired doneness, turning once (allow 10 to 12 minutes total for medium).
Brush occasionally with barbecue sauce after turning. Serve burgers on buns. Pass remaining sauce. Serves 4.

Hang on to those leftover heels of bread and make your own fine dry bread crumbs.
Just toast the bread till it's crisp and dry. Then, crush it with a rolling pin or whirl it in a food processor or blender. Each slice of bread makes about ¼ cup crumbs.

Beef-Vegetable Burgers

1 beaten egg
2 tablespoons milk
½ cup finely shredded carrot
¼ cup thinly sliced green onion
¼ cup toasted wheat germ
¼ teaspoon dried marjoram, crushed
¼ teaspoon salt
Dash pepper
1 pound lean ground beef

● In a medium mixing bowl combine egg and milk. Stir in carrot, green onion, wheat germ, marjoram, salt, and pepper. Add ground beef and mix well. Shape mixture into four ¾-inch-thick patties.
Place patties on an unheated rack in a broiler pan. Broil 3 to 4 inches from heat to desired doneness, turning once (allow about 12 minutes total for medium). *Or,* grill patties, on an uncovered grill, directly over *medium-hot* coals to desired doneness, turning once (allow 10 to 12 minutes total for medium).

1 cup shredded zucchini
1 cup alfalfa sprouts
¼ cup sunflower nuts
¼ cup creamy cucumber salad dressing

● Meanwhile, for vegetable topper, in a small mixing bowl combine zucchini, alfalfa sprouts, and sunflower nuts. Stir in salad dressing.

4 whole wheat hamburger buns, split and toasted

● Serve burgers on buns with the vegetable topper. Pass remaining topper. Makes 4 servings.

Play around with the flavor of the vegetable topper by switching salad dressings—creamy Italian, creamy bacon, creamy French, creamy buttermilk. Choose your favorite.

Souped-Up Cheeseburgers

1 beaten egg
¼ cup catsup
¼ cup fine dry bread crumbs
1 1-ounce envelope *regular* onion-mushroom soup mix
1½ pounds lean ground beef
6 slices American *or* cheddar cheese

● In a medium mixing bowl combine egg and catsup. Stir in bread crumbs and soup mix. Add ground beef and mix well. Shape meat mixture into six ¾-inch-thick patties.

Place patties on an unheated rack in a broiler pan. Broil 3 to 4 inches from heat to desired doneness, turning once (allow about 12 minutes total for medium). *Or,* grill patties, on an uncovered grill, directly over *medium-hot* coals to desired doneness, turning once (allow 10 to 12 minutes total for medium).

Top burgers with cheese. Heat just till cheese melts.

6 lettuce leaves
6 hamburger buns, split and toasted
6 tomato slices

● Serve burgers on lettuce-lined buns with tomato slices. Makes 6 servings.

Here's a question for trivia buffs. What was the first major hamburger chain in the U.S., and when did it open?
Answer: White Castle pushed the hamburger-on-a-bun into the limelight in 1921. The 2½-inch meat squares sold for 5¢ apiece!

Orange-Teriyaki Burgers

Teriyaki Sauce
¼ cup chopped water chestnuts
2 tablespoons thinly sliced green onion
1½ pounds lean ground beef

● In a medium mixing bowl combine ¼ *cup* Teriyaki Sauce, water chestnuts, and green onion. Add ground beef and mix well. Shape meat mixture into six ¾-inch-thick patties.

Place patties on an unheated rack in a broiler pan. Broil 3 to 4 inches from heat to desired doneness, turning once (allow about 12 minutes total for medium). *Or,* grill patties, on an uncovered grill, directly over *medium-hot* coals to desired doneness, turning once (allow 10 to 12 minutes total for medium).

Brush burgers occasionally with remaining Teriyaki Sauce after turning.

6 lettuce leaves
6 hamburger buns, split and toasted
1 orange, peeled and cut crosswise into 6 slices

● Serve burgers on lettuce-lined buns with orange slices. Makes 6 servings.

Our homemade Teriyaki Sauce adds a light orange flavor to the burger, but bottled teriyaki sauce makes a great-tasting burger, too.

Teriyaki Sauce: In a bowl combine 3 tablespoons *soy sauce,* 3 tablespoons *dry sherry,* 4 teaspoons frozen *orange juice concentrate,* and ¼ teaspoon ground *ginger.* Makes about ⅓ cup.

All-American Backyard Barbecue

Be it ever so humble, there's *nothing* quite like a backyard picnic starring the burger. Its smell wafting through the air can turn even an ordinary gathering into a special event. What's more, with our easy-to-do recipes, the food is a cinch.

So fire up the grill, call over your neighbors, and enjoy some of summer's best-loved foods. (See recipes on pages 16 through 19.)

MENU
Great Grilled Burgers
Curried Potato Salad
   or Cabbage Plus Slaw
Corn on the Cob
Marinated Tomato Wedges
Mock Summer Trifle

Great Grilled Burgers

Pictured on pages 14–15.

6 slices bacon	● In a large skillet cook bacon till crisp. Drain well, reserving drippings in skillet. Crumble bacon and set aside. Cook onion in reserved drippings till tender but not brown. Remove onion from skillet with a slotted spoon and drain well.
½ cup chopped onion	

For burgers on the double, shape ground meat into individual patties and freeze them ahead. The frozen patties will be easier to separate if you stack them between two layers of waxed paper. At mealtime, take out just the number of patties you need.

2 tablespoons catsup
1 tablespoon prepared horseradish
1 tablespoon prepared mustard
1½ pounds lean ground beef
6 lettuce leaves
6 hamburger buns, split and toasted

● In a medium mixing bowl combine catsup, horseradish, mustard, onion, and bacon. Add ground beef and mix well. Shape the meat mixture into six ¾-inch-thick patties.

Grill patties, on an uncovered grill, directly over *medium-hot* coals to desired doneness, turning once (allow 10 to 12 minutes total for medium).

Serve burgers on lettuce-lined buns. Makes 6 servings.

Fire Up

Tired of coals that go out? Food that's charred on the outside and raw inside? These fire-making pointers can help you eliminate all these grilling headaches.

● *Selecting the right number of coals.* Spread a single layer of briquettes about an inch beyond the food you're going to cook.

● *Lighting the fire.* To get the fire going faster, pile briquettes into a pyramid in the center of the firebox. If you're using self-lighting briquettes, simply ignite them with a long match. Otherwise, squirt briquettes with starter fluid, wait one minute, and carefully ignite (never squirt lighter fluid on hot coals).

● *Arranging the hot coals.* When the coals look ash gray, use long-handled tongs to spread them out for either direct or indirect cooking. (Regular-size burgers cook over direct heat; giant burgers over indirect heat.) For direct cooking, spread coals out in a single layer. For indirect cooking, arrange the coals in a circle, leaving the center open for a drip pan.

● *Testing the coals.* Test coals by holding your hand, palm down, where the food will be placed. Count the seconds (by saying "one thousand one," etc.). If you have to remove your hand after three seconds, coals are *medium-hot;* after four seconds, they're *medium.*

Corn on The Cob

Pictured on pages 14–15.

⅓ cup butter *or* margarine, softened 1 tablespoon snipped parsley ¼ to ½ teaspoon lemon pepper	● In a small mixing bowl combine butter or margarine, parsley, and lemon pepper.
6 fresh ears of corn	● Remove husks and silk from corn. Spread some of the butter mixture over each ear of corn. Cut six 18x12-inch pieces of *heavy* foil. Wrap each ear of corn in a piece of foil. Grill corn, on an uncovered grill, directly over *medium-hot* coals for 20 to 25 minutes or till tender, turning often. Makes 6 servings.

Add snap to your next six ears of corn with some of this piquant butter mixture.

Sassy Spread: Combine ⅓ cup *butter or margarine,* softened; 2 tablespoons *prepared mustard;* 2 tablespoons *prepared horseradish;* and 1 teaspoon *Worcestershire sauce.*

Marinated Tomato Wedges

Pictured on pages 14–15.

¼ cup salad oil ¼ cup white wine vinegar 2 tablespoons snipped parsley 2 tablespoons thinly sliced green onion 1 tablespoon mayonnaise *or* salad dressing 1 small clove garlic, minced ½ teaspoon dried dillweed ½ teaspoon dried basil, crushed ¼ teaspoon salt ¼ teaspoon dried oregano, crushed ⅛ teaspoon pepper	● For marinade, in a screw-top jar combine oil, vinegar, parsley, green onion, mayonnaise or salad dressing, garlic, dillweed, basil, salt, oregano, and pepper. Cover and shake well to mix.
6 medium tomatoes, cored and cut into wedges	● Place tomato wedges in a large mixing bowl and pour marinade over all. Stir gently. Cover and chill for several hours, gently stirring occasionally.
	● Just before serving, use a slotted spoon to remove tomatoes from marinade. Makes 6 servings.

MENU COUNTDOWN
1 Day Ahead:
Assemble Mock Summer Trifle, but wait till serving to put fruit on top. Cover; chill.
5–6 Hours Ahead:
Prepare Curried Potato Salad or Cabbage Plus Slaw. Cover and chill.
Prepare Marinated Tomato Wedges. Cover and chill. (Don't forget to stir the tomatoes once in a while.)
Assemble Corn on the Cob and set aside.
3 Hours Ahead:
Assemble Great Grilled Burgers. Cover and chill.
1 Hour Ahead:
Light the charcoal.
20–25 Minutes Ahead:
Start grilling the corn.
10–12 Minutes Ahead:
Start grilling the burgers.
After Meal:
Slice the remaining fruit and place it atop the trifle.

Curried Potato Salad

Pictured on pages 14–15.

6 medium potatoes (2
   pounds)
½ cup sliced radishes
⅓ cup sliced celery
2 tablespoons sliced green
   onion
2 tablespoons sweet pickle
   relish
3 hard-cooked eggs,
   coarsely chopped

● In a covered saucepan cook potatoes in boiling salted water for 25 to 30 minutes or till tender. Drain well. Peel and cube potatoes.
   Transfer potatoes to a large mixing bowl. Gently stir in radishes, celery, green onion, sweet pickle relish, and hard-cooked eggs. Cover and chill.

For picture-perfect potato salad, choose red tuber varieties such as Red Pontiacs, White Roses, or Irish Cobblers. They hold their shape better during boiling.

½ cup dairy sour cream
⅓ cup mayonnaise *or* salad
   dressing
1 tablespoon vinegar
1 to 1½ teaspoons curry
   powder
½ teaspoon salt
   Dash pepper

● For dressing, in a small mixing bowl combine sour cream, mayonnaise or salad dressing, vinegar, curry powder, salt, and pepper.
   Pour dressing over chilled potato mixture, then toss lightly to coat. Cover and chill thoroughly. Makes 6 servings.

Cabbage Plus Slaw

Pictured on pages 14–15.

3 cups shredded green
   cabbage
1 cup shredded red cabbage
1 cup alfalfa sprouts
1 cup shredded carrot
1 cup fresh pea pods *or*
   frozen pea pods, thawed

● In a large mixing bowl combine cabbage, alfalfa sprouts, carrot, and pea pods.

When your group eats with gusto, prepare *both* the Curried Potato Salad and the Cabbage Plus Slaw.

½ cup mayonnaise *or* salad
   dressing
1 tablespoon milk
2 teaspoons sugar
1 teaspoon celery seed
¼ teaspoon salt
½ cup broken walnuts

● For dressing, in a small mixing bowl combine mayonnaise or salad dressing, milk, sugar, celery seed, and salt. Pour dressing over cabbage mixture and toss lightly to coat. Cover and chill thoroughly.
   Just before serving, gently stir in walnuts. Makes 6 servings.

Mock Summer Trifle

Pictured on pages 14–15.

1 4-serving-size package *instant* vanilla *or* French vanilla pudding mix ¼ cup milk ¼ cup Amaretto liqueur	● Prepare pudding mix according to package directions, *except* add an additional ¼ cup milk. Stir Amaretto into pudding mixture.
1 frozen loaf pound cake, thawed and cut into ½-inch cubes 2 tablespoons strawberry preserves *or* jam 1½ cups sliced strawberries *and/or* peeled and sliced kiwi fruit	● To assemble trifle, place *half* of the cake cubes in a 2-quart soufflé dish or serving bowl, then dot with *half* of the strawberry preserves or jam. Spread *half* of the pudding mixture over preserves, then layer fruit atop pudding mixture. Repeat cake, preserves or jam, and pudding layers. Cover surface with clear plastic wrap. Chill 6 hours or overnight.
1½ cups sliced strawberries *and/or* peeled and sliced kiwi fruit	● Just before serving, arrange sliced fruit atop trifle. Makes 6 servings.

We trifled with this trifle so it's easier to prepare than the traditional dessert, but we left in every bit of lusciousness!

Iced Tea, Anyone?

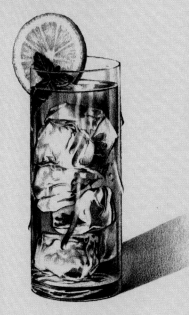

On sweltering days, nothing quenches your thirst faster than a tall, cool glass of iced tea. Just brew a glass or a big batch one of these ways.

● *Traditional brew:* Bring 4 cups of fresh, cold tap water to boiling. Pour water over 4 to 8 tea bags or 4 to 8 teaspoons of loose tea. Cover and let tea steep 3 to 5 minutes; remove tea bags or strain tea leaves. Hold tea at room temperature to prevent clouding.

● *Refrigerator brew:* Place 6 tea bags in a pitcher with 4 cups of fresh, cold water. Cover and refrigerate for several hours.

● *Sun brew:* Place 6 cups of cold water in a clear glass container. Add 4 tea bags, cover, and let stand in the full sun for 2 to 3 hours or to desired strength.

● *Fast brew:* Stir 1 rounded teaspoon of instant tea powder into a 6-ounce glass of cold water, then add ice. For a pitcherful, add 2 tablespoons of instant tea powder to each quart of cold water.

● **P.S.** Try any of the above brews with your favorite herbal tea.

Glazed Lamb Burgers

1 beaten egg
2 tablespoons plain yogurt
¼ cup fine dry bread crumbs
½ teaspoon dried mint,
   crushed
1 pound ground lamb
	● In a medium mixing bowl combine egg and yogurt. Stir in bread crumbs and mint. Add ground lamb and mix well. Shape meat mixture into four ¾-inch-thick patties.
	   Place patties on an unheated rack in a broiler pan. Broil 3 to 4 inches from heat to desired doneness, turning once (allow about 11 minutes total for medium). *Or,* grill patties, on an uncovered grill, directly over *medium-hot* coals to desired doneness, turning once (allow 10 to 12 minutes total for medium).

¼ cup apple jelly
1 tablespoon chopped
   pecans
1 tablespoon lemon juice
¼ teaspoon ground
   cinnamon
4 lettuce leaves
4 hamburger buns, split and
   toasted
	● Meanwhile, for glaze, combine apple jelly, pecans, lemon juice, and cinnamon. Spread glaze over burgers during the last minute of broiling or grilling.
	   Serve burgers on lettuce-lined buns. Makes 4 servings.

Here, the lamb's sweetness is accented with mint and apple jelly. Other recipes, such as Pesto Burgers on page 50, emphasize the robust qualities of the meat with parsley and garlic.

Burgers with Coriander Spread

1 beaten egg
⅓ cup quick-cooking rolled
   oats
¼ teaspoon salt
¼ teaspoon ground
   coriander
⅛ teaspoon pepper
1 pound ground lamb *or*
   pork
	● In a medium mixing bowl combine egg, rolled oats, salt, coriander, and pepper. Add ground meat and mix well. Shape meat mixture into four ¾-inch-thick patties.
	   Place patties on an unheated rack in a broiler pan. Broil 3 to 4 inches from the heat to desired doneness, turning once (allow about 11 minutes total for medium and about 14 minutes total for well-done). (Always cook pork till well-done.) *Or,* grill patties, on an uncovered grill, directly over *medium-hot* coals to desired doneness, turning once (allow 10 to 12 minutes total for medium and 12 to 15 minutes total for well-done).

Coriander Spread
   (see recipe, right)
4 hamburger buns, split and
   toasted
4 lettuce leaves
4 tomato slices
	● Spread Coriander Spread on both halves of split buns.
	   Serve burgers on lettuce-lined buns with tomato slices. Serves 4.

Coriander Spread: In a small mixing bowl stir together ¼ cup *mayonnaise or salad dressing,* ¼ cup sliced *green onion,* and ¼ teaspoon ground *coriander.* Makes about ⅓ cup.

Fish Patties With Herbed Tartar Sauce

2 beaten eggs
⅓ cup fine dry bread crumbs
½ teaspoon dried oregano, crushed
¼ teaspoon dried basil, crushed
2 cups flaked, cooked fish
½ cup finely crushed rich round crackers (12 crackers)
2 tablespoons cooking oil *or* shortening

● In a medium mixing bowl combine eggs, bread crumbs, oregano, and basil. Add fish and mix well. Shape fish mixture into four ¾-inch-thick patties. Coat patties with crushed crackers (see photo, below).

In a 10-inch skillet cook patties in hot oil or shortening over medium-low heat about 3 minutes on each side or till golden brown.

Leftover haddock or cod makes great patties. *Or,* steam a frozen one-pound package of fish fillets (see directions, page 61).

4 hamburger buns, split and toasted
Herbed Tartar Sauce

● Serve patties on buns with Herbed Tartar Sauce. Makes 4 servings.

Herbed Tartar Sauce: In a small mixing bowl combine ¼ cup *dairy sour cream,* ¼ cup *mayonnaise or salad dressing,* 1 tablespoon snipped *parsley,* 1 tablespoon sliced *green onion,* 1 tablespoon finely chopped *sweet pickle,* ¼ teaspoon *dry mustard,* ¼ teaspoon *paprika,* ⅛ teaspoon *salt,* and dash *pepper.* Makes about ½ cup.

Flake cooked fish by inserting a fork at a 45-degree angle. Twist the fork gently and the fish will break apart easily.

Put crushed crackers in a shallow dish or on a piece of waxed paper. Place a fish patty in the crumbs and twist it gently so the crumbs stick to the bottom. Turn the patty over and twist it again. Repeat with the rest of the fish patties.

Lobster Cakes Diablo

1 beaten egg
½ cup finely crushed rich round crackers
1 teaspoon prepared mustard
¼ teaspoon ground red pepper
1 6½-ounce can lobster meat *or* one 6-ounce can crabmeat, drained, flaked, and cartilage removed
2 tablespoons cooking oil *or* shortening

● In a medium mixing bowl combine egg, crushed crackers, mustard, and red pepper. Add lobster or crabmeat and mix well. Shape lobster mixture into two ½- to ¾-inch-thick patties. Cover and chill patties for at least 30 minutes.

In a 10-inch skillet cook patties in hot oil or shortening over medium heat for 3 to 4 minutes on each side or till golden brown. Drain patties on paper towels.

Diablo means "devil" in Spanish, but "spicy" in culinary lingo. The devilish seasonings in this fish patty are mustard and ground red pepper.

2 lettuce leaves
2 whole wheat hamburger buns, split and toasted
2 tomato slices

● Serve patties on lettuce-lined buns with tomato slices. Makes 2 servings.

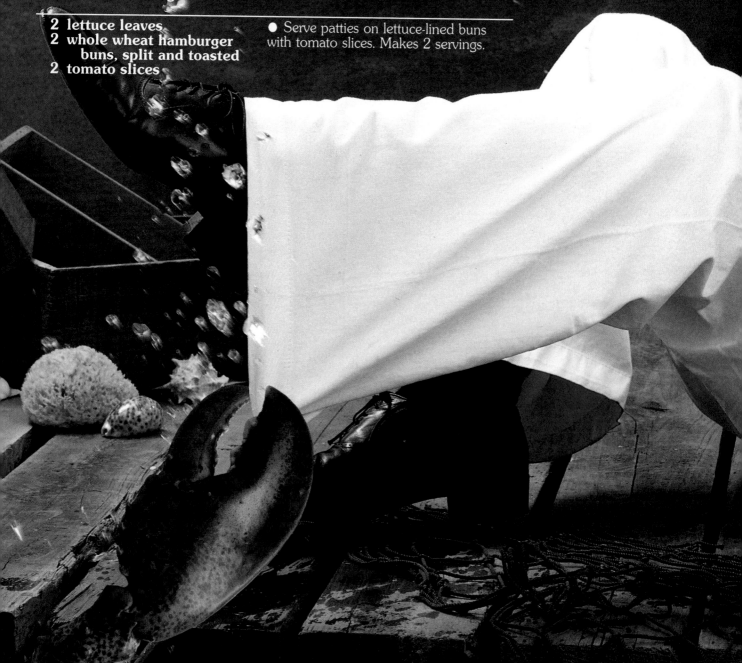

Easy Salmon Patties

1 beaten egg
¼ cup milk
½ cup finely crushed saltine crackers (14 crackers)
½ teaspoon dried dillweed
¼ teaspoon paprika
1 7¾-ounce can salmon, drained, flaked, and skin and bones removed
4 slices cheddar, Swiss, *or* American cheese

● In a medium mixing bowl combine egg and milk. Stir in crushed crackers, dillweed, and paprika. Add salmon and mix well. Cover and chill for 30 minutes. Shape salmon mixture into four ½-inch-thick patties.

Place patties in a well-greased shallow baking pan. Broil 3 to 4 inches from the heat for 6 to 8 minutes, turning once. Top patties with cheese. Heat just till cheese melts.

Chum, pink, silver, king, chinook, and sockeye—all different kinds of canned salmons. Choose one of the less expensive kinds (chum or pink) for patties, casseroles, and soups.

4 lettuce leaves
4 hamburger buns, split and toasted
4 tomato slices

● Serve patties on lettuce-lined buns with tomato slices. Makes 4 servings.

Off-the-Shelf Turkey Burgers

1 beaten egg
1 tablespoon dried parsley flakes
1 tablespoon minced dried onion
1 teaspoon instant chicken bouillon granules
½ cup shredded carrot
1 pound ground raw turkey
1 cup herb-seasoned stuffing mix, slightly crushed

● In a medium mixing bowl combine egg, parsley flakes, onion, and bouillon granules. Stir in carrot. Add ground turkey and mix well. Shape meat mixture into four ¾-inch-thick patties. Coat patties with crushed stuffing mix.

Place patties on a greased, unheated rack in a broiler pan. Broil 3 to 4 inches from the heat about 14 minutes total or till well-done, turning once. (Always cook turkey till well-done.)

Save broiler pan cleanup by frying the turkey patties in a 10-inch skillet. Cook the patties over medium heat in about 2 tablespoons hot *oil* for 5 to 6 minutes on each side or till well-done.

4 lettuce leaves
4 hamburger buns, split and toasted
¼ cup cranberry-orange relish

● Serve burgers on lettuce-lined buns with relish. Makes 4 servings.

Curried Turkey Burgers

2 tablespoons finely chopped onion
1 to 1½ teaspoons curry powder
2 teaspoons butter *or* margarine
1 teaspoon all-purpose flour
¾ cup plain yogurt

● For curry sauce, in a small saucepan cook onion and curry powder in butter or margarine till onion is tender. Remove from the heat. Stir flour into yogurt, then stir into onion mixture.

1 beaten egg
⅓ cup quick-cooking rolled oats
2 tablespoons snipped parsley
¼ teaspoon salt
1 pound ground raw turkey *or* lamb

● In a medium mixing bowl combine egg and *2 tablespoons* curry sauce. Stir in rolled oats, parsley, and salt. Add ground meat and mix well. Shape meat mixture into four ¾-inch-thick patties.

Place patties on an unheated rack in a broiler pan. (Lightly grease rack if using turkey.) Broil 3 to 4 inches from the heat to desired doneness, turning once (allow about 14 minutes total for well-done and 11 minutes total for medium). (Always cook turkey till well-done.) *Or,* grill patties, on an uncovered grill, directly over *medium-hot* coals to desired doneness, turning once (allow 12 to 15 minutes for well-done and 10 to 12 minutes for medium). (Brush cold grill rack with cooking oil if using turkey.)

2 tablespoons finely chopped chutney
4 hamburger buns, split and toasted

● Meanwhile, stir chutney into remaining curry sauce. Cook and stir just till heated through *(do not boil).*
Serve burgers on buns with sauce. Makes 4 servings.

Here's our favorite blend for homemade curry powder:

In a blender container place 4½ teaspoons ground *coriander,* 2 teaspoons ground *turmeric,* 1¼ teaspoons *cumin seed,* ½ to 1 teaspoon whole *black pepper,* ½ to 1 teaspoon crushed *red pepper,* ½ teaspoon whole *cardamom seed* (without pods), ½ inch stick *cinnamon,* ¼ teaspoon whole *cloves,* and ¼ teaspoon ground *ginger.* Cover and grind for 1 to 2 minutes or till mixture is a fine powder. Store the spice mixture in an airtight container in a cool, dry place. Makes about ¼ cup.

Talkin' Turkey

A trip to the meat counter used to mean a choice between ground beef, pork, or lamb. But ground raw turkey has made its way into the meat case along with these old standbys.

You'll find ground turkey packaged fresh, but it's also available frozen in 1-pound tubes. The moisture content from package to package can vary enough to affect recipes. If the turkey seems wet, decrease the liquid in the recipe by 1 or 2 tablespoons.

Herbed Veggie Burgers

3 cups water
¾ cup dry lentils

● In a medium saucepan bring water and lentils to boiling. Reduce the heat and simmer, covered, about 35 minutes or till tender. Drain and mash lentils.

2 beaten eggs
½ cup toasted pumpkin seed, chopped
½ cup fine dry bread crumbs
¼ cup chopped walnuts
¼ cup finely chopped green pepper
¼ cup finely chopped onion
¼ cup snipped parsley
½ teaspoon dried oregano, crushed
½ teaspoon dried basil, crushed
¼ teaspoon salt
¼ teaspoon pepper
1 tablespoon butter *or* margarine
3 large whole wheat pita bread rounds, halved crosswise
6 tomato slices
  Alfalfa sprouts
  Dairy sour cream *or* plain yogurt (optional)

● In a medium mixing bowl combine eggs, pumpkin seed, bread crumbs, nuts, green pepper, onion, parsley, oregano, basil, salt, pepper, and mashed lentils. Shape the lentil mixture into 6 oval patties, each about 5 inches long and ½ inch thick.

In a 12-inch skillet cook patties in butter or margarine over medium-low heat about 4 minutes on each side or till golden brown.

Serve patties in pita halves with tomato slices, alfalfa sprouts, and sour cream or yogurt, if desired. Serves 6.

Snipping fresh herbs such as parsley is a snap. Just put the herb in a 1-cup measure and snip it with kitchen shears.

Sweet and Sour Relish Burgers

2 slices bacon
⅓ cup chopped red *or* green sweet pepper
¼ cup chopped onion
1½ cups shredded cabbage
¼ cup shredded carrot
2 tablespoons brown sugar
2 tablespoons vinegar
2 tablespoons cold water
1 teaspoon cornstarch

● For relish, in a 10-inch skillet cook bacon till crisp. Drain bacon, reserving 1 tablespoon drippings. Crumble bacon.

In the skillet cook sweet pepper and onion in drippings till tender but not brown. Stir in cabbage, carrot, brown sugar, and vinegar. Cover and cook for 5 minutes. Combine water and cornstarch; add to skillet. Cook and stir till thickened and bubbly, then cook and stir 2 minutes more. Stir in bacon. Heat through.

You can't fit a square peg in a round hole—or a round burger in an oblong pita bread pocket!

To serve burgers in pita bread, shape the meat into oval patties about 5 inches long and ½ inch thick.

1 pound ground pork *or* raw turkey
¼ teaspoon salt
2 large pita bread rounds, halved crosswise

● Meanwhile, for burgers, shape meat into 4 oval patties, each about 5 inches long and ½ inch thick. Sprinkle with salt.

Place patties on an unheated rack in a broiler pan. (Lightly grease rack if using turkey.) Broil 3 to 4 inches from the heat about 11 minutes total or till well-done, turning once. (Always cook pork and turkey till well-done.) *Or,* grill patties, on an uncovered grill, directly over *medium-hot* coals for 8 to 10 minutes total or till well-done, turning once. (Brush cold grill rack with cooking oil if using turkey.)

Serve burgers in pita halves with relish. Makes 4 servings.

Five-Spice Pork Burgers

1 beaten egg
2 tablespoons soy sauce
¼ cup fine dry bread crumbs
2 tablespoons finely chopped onion
¼ teaspoon five-spice powder
1 pound ground pork

● In a medium mixing bowl combine egg and soy sauce. Stir in bread crumbs, onion, and five-spice powder. Add pork and mix well. Shape meat mixture into four ¾-inch-thick patties.

Place patties on an unheated rack in a broiler pan. Broil 3 to 4 inches from the heat about 14 minutes total or till well-done, turning once. *Or,* grill patties, on an uncovered grill, directly over *medium-hot* coals for 12 to 15 minutes total or till well-done, turning once. (Always cook pork till well-done.)

Most supermarkets carry Oriental five-spice powder these days, but you may already have all the spices you need on hand to make your own. Here's how:

Stir together 1 teaspoon ground *cinnamon;* 1 teaspoon crushed *aniseed or* 1 star *anise,* crushed; ¼ teaspoon crushed *fennel seed;* ¼ teaspoon freshly ground *black pepper or Szechuan pepper;* and ⅛ teaspoon ground *cloves.* Store tightly covered. Makes about 1 tablespoon.

4 hamburger buns, split and toasted
4 tomato slices
Alfalfa sprouts (optional)

● Serve burgers on buns with tomato slices and alfalfa sprouts, if desired. Makes 4 servings.

Breakfast Burgers

¾ **pound ground turkey sausage** *or* **bulk pork sausage**
3 **slices American cheese, quartered**

● Shape sausage into six ¼-inch-thick patties. Place patties on an unheated rack in a broiler pan. Broil 3 to 4 inches from the heat about 6 minutes total or till well-done, turning once. Top each burger with 2 cheese quarters. Heat just till cheese melts.

3 **eggs**
2 **tablespoons milk**
⅛ **teaspoon salt**
 Dash pepper
1 **tablespoon butter** *or* **margarine**
 Cornmeal-Herb Biscuits, split

● Meanwhile, in a small bowl beat together eggs, milk, salt, and pepper.
 In an 8-inch skillet cook and stir eggs in hot butter or margarine, cooking just till set. Place some of the scrambled eggs atop each biscuit bottom. Top with burgers and biscuit tops. Serves 6.

Cornmeal-Herb Biscuits: In a medium mixing bowl stir together 1 cup *all-purpose flour,* ¼ cup *yellow cornmeal,* 1½ teaspoons *baking powder,* ¼ teaspoon *salt,* ¼ teaspoon *baking soda,* and ¼ teaspoon dried *oregano, basil, or marjoram,* crushed.
 In a small mixing bowl combine one 8-ounce carton dairy *sour cream* and 2 tablespoons *milk.* Make a well in the center of the dry ingredients, then add sour cream mixture. Stir just till the dough clings together.
 Knead gently on a lightly floured surface for 10 to 12 strokes. Roll or pat to a ½-inch thickness. Cut with a 3-inch biscuit cutter, rerolling as necessary.
 Transfer to a lightly greased baking sheet. Bake in a 375° oven about 18 minutes or till golden. Makes 6 biscuits.

Kneading 10 to 12 strokes—no less and no more—is the secret to turning out first-rate biscuits every time. Too little kneading turns out biscuits that are small and round; the other extreme gives you biscuits that are tough and dry, with a peak on top.

Rhine Burgers

1 beaten egg
2 tablespoons beer
¼ cup fine dry rye bread
  crumbs
½ teaspoon caraway seed
1 pound lean ground beef
4 slices Muenster cheese
  (2 ounces)

---

8 slices rye *or* pumpernickel
  bread, toasted
½ cup sauerkraut, well
  drained
  German Potato Salad
  (see recipe, opposite)

● In a medium mixing bowl combine egg and beer. Stir in bread crumbs and caraway seed. Add ground beef and mix well. Shape into 4 oval patties, each about 5 inches long and ½ inch thick.

Place patties on an unheated rack in a broiler pan. Broil 3 to 4 inches from heat to desired doneness, turning once (allow about 9 minutes total for medium). Top with cheese. Heat just till cheese melts.

● Serve burgers on toasted bread with sauerkraut. Serve burgers with German Potato Salad. Makes 4 servings.

Oompah-pah, oompah-pah —that's the sound of Bavarian bands playing at Munich's Oktoberfest!

Ten million people roll into Munich annually to drink, sing, and dance. Huge tents are set up to serve mountains of food, along with steins of foaming beer.

Throw your own Oktoberfest and serve this Rhine Burger, German Potato Salad, and lots of beer.

● You probably won't find burgers exactly like the ones in this section in China, Greece, or Rome. We've borrowed the herbs, spices, and native ingredients of each area and created our own ethnic versions.

German Potato Salad

1 pound tiny new potatoes
***or* medium potatoes**

● Scrub potatoes. Remove a narrow strip of peel around center of each new potato or quarter each medium potato. Cook potatoes, covered, in boiling salted water till tender (allow 10 to 15 minutes for tiny new potatoes or 20 to 25 minutes for quartered medium potatoes). Drain well.

Germany is known as a nation of potato eaters, but that hasn't always been true.

3 slices bacon
½ cup chopped onion
¼ cup chopped green pepper
1 tablespoon all-purpose flour
1 tablespoon sugar
½ teaspoon celery seed
Dash pepper
½ cup water
¼ cup vinegar
1 hard-cooked egg, sliced

● Meanwhile, in a medium saucepan cook bacon till crisp. Drain bacon, reserving 2 tablespoons drippings. Crumble bacon and set aside.

In the saucepan cook onion and green pepper in reserved drippings till tender but not brown. Stir in flour, sugar, celery seed, and pepper. Add water and vinegar. Cook and stir till thickened and bubbly. Stir in bacon and potatoes. Cook about 5 minutes more or till heated through, tossing lightly. Garnish with egg slices. Serve at once. Makes 4 servings.

King Frederick the Great tried to persuade his subjects to grow and eat potatoes. The peasants, however, thought they were poisonous. Eventually the king dispatched troops to distribute the potatoes. The forcible persuasion worked—the potatoes were planted and grew to become a mainstay of the German diet.

Tabbouleh

1 cup bulgur wheat
1 small tomato, chopped
½ cup shredded carrot
¼ cup snipped parsley
2 tablespoons thinly sliced green onion
1 tablespoon snipped fresh mint *or* 1 teaspoon dried mint, crushed
3 tablespoons olive *or* cooking oil
3 tablespoons lemon juice
Lettuce leaves
Tomato rose (optional)

● In a medium saucepan combine bulgur and 2 cups *water*. Bring to boiling. Remove from the heat. Let stand, covered, for 20 minutes. Drain.

In a medium mixing bowl stir together tomato, carrot, parsley, green onion, mint, and ¼ teaspoon *salt*. Stir in bulgur. Combine olive or cooking oil and lemon juice. Toss with bulgur mixture. Cover and chill thoroughly.

Serve in a lettuce-lined bowl. Garnish with a tomato rose, if desired. Makes 6 to 8 servings.

Do you know any two people who make potato salad alike? Probably not—and the same thing goes for Tabbouleh. It's a traditional Middle Eastern salad that always has bulgur wheat and parsley in it, but the ratio and seasonings vary from cook to cook.

Middle Eastern Burgers With Tahini Sauce

Tahini
⅓ cup water
3 tablespoons lemon juice
1 clove garlic, minced

● Prepare Tahini. For sauce, in a small saucepan stir together Tahini, water, lemon juice, and garlic. Cook and stir till heated through. Keep sauce warm.

Middle Eastern cooks use tahini the way Americans use catsup. They depend on this sesame seed sauce to flavor fish, meat, vegetables, salads, and sandwiches.

¼ cup fine dry bread crumbs
1½ pounds ground lamb *or* lean beef

● In a medium mixing bowl combine fine dry bread crumbs and *3 tablespoons* sauce. Add ground meat and mix well. Shape mixture into 6 oval patties, each about 5 inches long and ½ inch thick.

Place patties on an unheated rack in a broiler pan. Broil 3 to 4 inches from heat to desired doneness, turning once (allow about 9 minutes total for medium).

6 lettuce leaves
3 large pita bread rounds, halved crosswise
Thinly sliced cucumber (optional)
Tabbouleh (see recipe, left)

● Serve burgers in lettuce-lined pita halves with sauce and cucumber slices, if desired. Serve burgers with Tabbouleh. Makes 6 servings.

Tahini: Place 1 cup lightly toasted *sesame seed* and ¼ teaspoon *salt* in a food processor or blender container. Cover and process or blend for 3 to 5 minutes or till a butter forms, stopping occasionally to scrape down sides of container. Add 1 tablespoon *olive or cooking oil*. Cover and process or blend till smooth. Makes ½ cup.

Maui Burgers

¼ cup finely chopped green pepper
2 tablespoons finely chopped onion
2 tablespoons chopped macadamia nuts *or* peanuts
1 tablespoon soy sauce
1 teaspoon prepared mustard
⅛ teaspoon ground ginger
1 pound ground pork, raw turkey, *or* lean beef

● In a medium mixing bowl combine green pepper, onion, nuts, soy sauce, mustard, and ginger. Add ground meat and mix well. Shape meat mixture into four ¾-inch-thick patties.

Place patties on an unheated rack in a broiler pan. (Lightly grease the rack if using turkey.) Broil 3 to 4 inches from the heat to desired doneness, turning once (allow about 14 minutes total for well-done and about 12 minutes total for medium). (Always cook pork and turkey till well-done.)

In the early 1900s, farmers were convinced that macadamia nuts would never be profitable because the trees took 18 years to bear nuts. How wrong they were! The rich, almondlike flavor of the nuts is so irresistible that the demand for them has skyrocketed.

4 hamburger buns, split and toasted
Tropical Fruit Salad (see recipe, below)

● Serve burgers on buns with Tropical Fruit Salad. Makes 4 servings.

Tropical Fruit Salad

1 banana, bias-sliced, *or* 1 cup fresh strawberries, sliced
Lemon juice
Torn curly endive
1 grapefruit, peeled and sectioned
1 orange, peeled and sliced crosswise
1 papaya, sliced; 1 cup honeydew melon balls; *or* one 8-ounce can pineapple slices (juice pack), drained

● If using banana slices, toss with lemon juice to prevent browning (if not using bananas, omit lemon juice).

Line a serving platter with endive. Arrange banana slices or strawberries, grapefruit sections, orange slices, and papaya slices, melon balls, or pineapple slices on platter. Cover and chill for at least 2 hours.

Our secret salad ingredient is ripe, buttery-tasting papaya. Choose yellowish ones that yield slightly to pressure. Small spots on the skin are a sign of ripeness. Let green papayas stand at room temperature out of direct sunlight to ripen, then refrigerate them.

Tropical Salad Dressing
2 tablespoons toasted coconut

● Just before serving, drizzle Tropical Salad Dressing over fruit and sprinkle with coconut. Makes 4 servings.

Tropical Salad Dressing: In a small bowl stir together ¼ cup *plain yogurt* and 2 teaspoons *sugar.* If necessary, stir in about 1 tablespoon *fruit juice or milk* to make of drizzling consistency. Makes about ¼ cup.

Indian Burgers

Honeyed Apple Rings
1 beaten egg
2 tablespoons applesauce
¼ cup fine dry bread crumbs
1½ teaspoons curry powder
1 teaspoon prepared mustard
¼ teaspoon crushed red pepper
¼ teaspoon salt
1 pound lean ground beef or lamb

● Prepare Honeyed Apple Rings and set aside. In a medium mixing bowl combine egg and applesauce. Stir in bread crumbs, curry powder, mustard, red pepper, and salt. Add ground meat and mix well. Shape meat mixture into four ¾-inch-thick patties.

Place patties on an unheated rack in a broiler pan. Broil 3 to 4 inches from heat to desired doneness, turning once (allow about 12 minutes total for medium).

Applesauce or chutney are great stand-ins for the apple rings.

4 lettuce leaves
4 hamburger buns, split and toasted
Gingered Cauliflower Stir-Fry (see recipe, below)

● Serve burgers on lettuce-lined buns with Honeyed Apple Rings. Serve with Gingered Cauliflower Stir-Fry. Serves 4.

Honeyed Apple Rings: Wash and core 1 small *apple*. Cut crosswise into 4 rings. In a small saucepan stir together 1 tablespoon *honey*, 2 teaspoons *vinegar*, ⅛ teaspoon ground *cinnamon*, and dash *salt*. Bring to boiling. Reduce heat and add apple rings. Cover and cook about 5 minutes or till rings are translucent.

Gingered Cauliflower Stir-Fry

1 tablespoon cooking oil
2 teaspoons grated gingerroot
½ of a medium head cauliflower, thinly sliced (2¼ cups)
1 medium red *or* green sweet pepper, cut into ¾-inch pieces (¾ cup)

● Preheat a wok or large skillet over high heat, then add oil. (Add more oil, as necessary, during cooking.)

Stir-fry gingerroot in hot oil for 15 seconds. Add cauliflower and stir-fry for 3 minutes. Add sweet pepper and stir-fry about 2 minutes more or till vegetables are crisp-tender.

You'll need about an inch of fresh gingerroot to yield the 2 teaspoons of grated gingerroot.

1 medium tomato, cut into thin wedges
3 tablespoons coarsely chopped cashews
2 tablespoons snipped parsley *or* coriander

● Remove from the heat. Stir in tomato and cashews. Sprinkle with parsley or coriander. Makes 4 servings.

U.S.A. Burgers

1 **beaten egg**
2 **tablespoons catsup**
¼ **cup fine dry bread crumbs**
1 **tablespoon prepared mustard**
¼ **teaspoon onion powder**
⅛ **teaspoon garlic powder**
  Dash pepper
1 **pound lean ground beef**
4 **slices bacon, cut in half crosswise**
4 **slices cheddar cheese**
4 **slices jalapeño pepper cheese**

● In a medium mixing bowl combine egg and catsup. Stir in bread crumbs, mustard, onion powder, garlic powder, and pepper. Add ground beef and mix well. Shape meat mixture into four ¾-inch-thick patties.

Place patties on an unheated rack in a broiler pan. Broil 3 to 4 inches from the heat to desired doneness, turning once (allow about 12 minutes total for medium). To cook bacon, place it on the broiler rack beside patties during the last 5 to 6 minutes of broiling; drain bacon.

Top burgers with a slice of each cheese. Heat just till cheese melts.

4 **lettuce leaves**
4 **hamburger buns, split and toasted**
4 **tomato slices**
4 **onion slices**

● Serve each burger on a lettuce-lined bun with a tomato and onion slice and 2 bacon pieces. Makes 4 servings.

Although U.S. cooks claim burgers as all-American, the history of burgers really goes back to the 13th century Tartars of central Asia.

Because the Tartars were herders constantly on the move, they rarely built a fire at mealtime. Instead they simply shredded raw lamb into mounds or patties for a meal.

After the Tartars swept through Russia, the Russians developed their own version using beef that's now known as steak or beef Tartar.

Home Fries

3 medium potatoes ¼ teaspoon salt ¼ teaspoon pepper	● In a medium saucepan cook potatoes, covered, in boiling water for 20 to 25 minutes or just till tender. Drain and cool slightly. Cut potatoes into ¼-inch-thick slices. Sprinkle with salt and pepper.	
3 tablespoons cooking oil *or* shortening ¼ cup thinly sliced green onion	● In a 10-inch skillet cook potato slices, uncovered, in hot oil or shortening over medium heat for 12 to 15 minutes or till brown, turning occasionally. Add green onion during the last 2 to 3 minutes. Makes 4 servings.	

Fried potatoes are truly an international favorite. Americans douse them with catsup. The French serve them with salt and pepper. The Dutch and Belgians offer them with mustard-mayonnaise. And the English prefer them with a touch of vinegar.

Burgers O'Malley

½ of a 12-ounce package
   frozen shredded hash
   brown potatoes, thawed
   (1½ cups)
2 tablespoons butter or
   margarine
¼ cup sliced green onion
¼ cup chopped green pepper

● Chop potatoes slightly. Melt butter or margarine in an 8-inch skillet. Add potatoes, onion, and green pepper. Cook, covered, over medium-low heat about 10 minutes or till potatoes are tender, stirring occasionally.

Pickling beef brisket in a strong brine flavored with allspice, cloves, peppercorns, and garlic makes fantastic corned beef.

1 beaten egg
¼ teaspoon garlic salt
1 12-ounce can corned beef,
   finely chopped

● In a medium mixing bowl combine egg and garlic salt. Stir in potato mixture. Add corned beef and mix well. Cover and chill for 1 hour. Shape corned beef mixture into six ¾-inch-thick patties.
   Place the corned beef patties in a 12x7½x2-inch baking dish. Bake, uncovered, in a 350° oven for 20 to 25 minutes or till heated through.

6 hamburger buns, split and
   toasted
   Mustard
6 green pepper rings
   Saucy Cabbage
   (see recipe, below)

● Serve burgers on buns with mustard and green pepper rings. Serve with Saucy Cabbage. Makes 6 servings.

Saucy Cabbage

6 cups coarsely chopped
   cabbage
1 cup water
¼ teaspoon salt

● In a large saucepan combine cabbage, water, and salt. Bring to boiling. Reduce the heat and cook, covered, for 6 to 8 minutes or till tender, stirring occasionally. Drain well.

No blarney here—you can plan on one small head of cabbage yielding the six cups of coarsely chopped cabbage you need for this Irish-style side dish.

2 tablespoons butter or
   margarine
2 tablespoons all-purpose
   flour
½ teaspoon caraway seed
   Dash pepper
1 cup milk
½ cup shredded American
   cheese (2 ounces)

● Meanwhile, for sauce melt the butter or margarine in a medium saucepan. Stir in flour, caraway seed, and pepper. Add milk all at once. Cook and stir till thickened and bubbly. Remove from the heat. Add cheese, stirring till melted. Stir drained cabbage into cheese sauce, then transfer to a 1-quart casserole.

1 tablespoon butter or
   margarine, melted
¾ cup soft bread crumbs
   (1 slice)

● Toss melted butter or margarine with bread crumbs. Sprinkle over cabbage mixture. Bake, uncovered, in a 350° oven about 20 minutes or till heated through. Makes 6 servings.

Burgers Roma

1 beaten egg
¼ cup fine dry bread crumbs
1 teaspoon dried Italian
    seasoning, crushed
¼ teaspoon garlic salt
1 pound lean ground beef
½ pound bulk Italian
    sausage

● In a medium mixing bowl combine egg, bread crumbs, Italian seasoning, and garlic salt. Add ground meats and mix well. Shape meat mixture into six ¾-inch-thick patties.

Place patties on an unheated rack in a broiler pan. Broil 3 to 4 inches from the heat for 12 to 14 minutes total or till well-done, turning once.

The little bit of Italian sausage in this burger really peps it up!

3 cups shredded lettuce
  Risotto Primavera (see
    recipe, below)

● Serve burgers on shredded lettuce with Risotto Primavera. Serves 6.

Risotto Primavera

¼ cup chopped onion
1 tablespoon butter or
    margarine
2 cups chicken broth
¾ cup short, medium, or
    long grain rice
1½ teaspoons snipped fresh
    basil, rosemary, or
    thyme, or ½ teaspoon
    dried basil, rosemary, or
    thyme, crushed
¼ teaspoon salt
⅛ teaspoon pepper

● In a medium saucepan cook onion in butter or margarine till tender but not brown. Stir in broth, rice, desired herb, salt, and pepper. Bring to boiling. Reduce the heat and simmer, covered, for 15 minutes (do not lift cover).

In parts of Italy, rice vies with pasta for star billing. And one of the most popular rice dishes is risotto (ruh-SOT-o).

For perfect risotto, the rice must simmer, tightly covered, in a seasoned broth till the mixture is creamy and the rice is tender, but still slightly firm (what Italians refer to as "al dente").

1 small yellow summer
    squash or zucchini,
    halved lengthwise and
    sliced into ¼-inch-thick
    pieces
1 cup broccoli flowerets

● Meanwhile, cook summer squash or zucchini and broccoli, uncovered, in a small amount of boiling water for 5 to 8 minutes or till vegetables are crisp-tender. Drain.

1 large tomato, peeled,
    seeded, and chopped

● Remove rice from the heat. Stir in cooked vegetables. Cover and let stand for 5 to 8 minutes or just till rice is tender. Stir in tomato. Serve immediately. Makes 6 servings.

Peking Burgers

1 beaten egg
1 tablespoon soy sauce
1 teaspoon sesame oil
¼ cup fine dry bread crumbs
1 tablespoon sesame seed, toasted
½ teaspoon Roasted Szechuan Salt-Pepper
1½ pounds lean ground beef

● Combine egg, soy sauce, and sesame oil. Stir in bread crumbs, sesame seed, and Roasted Szechuan Salt-Pepper. Add ground beef and mix well. Shape meat mixture into six ¾-inch-thick patties.

Place patties on an unheated rack in a broiler pan. Broil 3 to 4 inches from the heat to desired doneness, turning once (allow about 12 minutes total for medium).

6 hamburger buns, split and toasted
1½ cups shredded Chinese cabbage *or* cabbage
Plum sauce
Fried Rice (see recipe, below)

● Serve burgers on buns with shredded cabbage and plum sauce. Serve burgers with Fried Rice. Makes 6 servings

Roasted Szechuan Salt-Pepper: In a heavy skillet combine 3 tablespoons *salt* and 1 tablespoon *Szechuan peppercorns.* Cook and stir over medium heat for 5 to 7 minutes or till peppercorns begin to smoke slightly and salt is lightly browned. Remove from the heat. Cool.

With a mortar and pestle or rolling pin, crush salt and peppercorns. Pass salt-peppercorn mixture through a sieve to remove peppercorn husks. Store tightly covered. Makes about ¼ cup.

You'll find plum sauce in grocery stores or Oriental markets. Or, mix up this homemade version.

Plum Sauce: Combine ½ cup *plum preserves,* 2 teaspoons *vinegar,* 1½ teaspoons *brown sugar,* ¼ to ½ teaspoon crushed *red pepper,* ¼ teaspoon ground *ginger,* and 1 small clove *garlic,* minced. Bring to boiling, stirring constantly. Remove from heat and cool slightly. Chill, covered, overnight to blend seasonings. Reheat before serving. Makes about ½ cup.

Fried Rice

2 tablespoons soy sauce
1 tablespoon dry sherry
½ teaspoon sugar

● For sauce, in a small mixing bowl combine soy sauce, dry sherry, and sugar. Set aside.

2 tablespoons cooking oil
2 beaten eggs
1 teaspoon grated gingerroot
1 medium carrot, thinly bias sliced (½ cup)
3 green onions, bias-sliced into 1-inch lengths (½ cup)

● Preheat a wok or large skillet over medium heat, then add *1 tablespoon* oil. Add eggs. Cook according to directions at right. Remove strips from wok.

Return wok or skillet to heat. Add remaining oil to hot wok (add more oil as necessary during cooking). Stir-fry gingerroot in hot oil for 15 seconds. Add carrot and stir-fry for 2 to 3 minutes. Add green onions. Stir-fry for 1 to 1½ minutes or till vegetables are crisp-tender.

2 cups cooked rice, chilled
1 8-ounce can sliced water chestnuts, drained

● Stir rice, water chestnuts, and sauce mixture into wok. Cook and stir for 1 minute. Gently stir in egg strips. Cover and cook for 1 minute. Serves 6.

To cook the eggs as shown at right, pour beaten eggs into hot wok or skillet. Lift and tilt the wok to form a thin layer of egg on the bottom and partially up the sides of the wok. Cook, without stirring, for 2 to 3 minutes or just till set. Remove the wok or skillet from the heat. Use a spatula to cut the cooked eggs into bite-size strips.

Mediterranean Burgers

⅓ cup plain yogurt
¼ cup fine dry bread crumbs
¾ teaspoon snipped fresh mint *or* ¼ teaspoon dried mint, crushed
½ teaspoon salt
¼ teaspoon ground allspice
1½ pounds ground lamb

● In a medium mixing bowl combine yogurt, bread crumbs, mint, salt, and allspice. Add ground lamb and mix well. Shape mixture into 6 oval patties, each about 5 inches long and ½ inch thick.

Place patties on an unheated rack in a broiler pan. Broil 3 to 4 inches from heat to desired doneness, turning once (allow about 9 minutes total for medium).

3 large pita bread rounds, halved crosswise
6 tomato slices
Plain yogurt (optional)
Greek Salad (see recipe, below)

● Serve burgers in pita halves with tomato slices. Dollop with yogurt, if desired. Serve with Greek Salad. Makes 6 servings.

Greeks call it *pita;* Turks, *pide;* Iranians, *peda;* and Americans, *pocket bread.* This unleavened bread has spilled over from the ovens of the Mediterranean and the Middle East right into our supermarkets!

Stuff pita bread's built-in pocket with meat, vegetables, salads, cheese, or eggs to make a meal-in-hand. Or, use it to scoop up food or dunk into soups or sauces.

Greek Salad

½ of a medium head romaine, torn (3 cups)
1 small cucumber *or* zucchini, sliced
3 radishes, sliced
1 tablespoon sliced green onion
¼ cup crumbled feta cheese
¼ cup pitted ripe olives

● In a large serving bowl combine torn romaine, cucumber or zucchini, radishes, and green onion. Top with feta cheese and olives. Cover and chill.

No meal in Greece or Turkey is complete without a giant tossed salad—one that's full of fresh vegetables, tossed with a simple oil and vinegar (or lemon juice) dressing, and topped with feta cheese.

¼ cup olive *or* salad oil
2 tablespoons wine vinegar
¼ teaspoon dried oregano, crushed
Dash pepper
1 small clove garlic, minced

● For dressing, in a screwtop jar combine oil, vinegar, oregano, pepper, and garlic. Cover and shake well to mix. Chill thoroughly.

● Just before serving, shake dressing again, then pour over salad. Toss lightly to coat. Makes 6 servings.

Burgers Français

1½ pounds lean ground beef
Salt
Pepper

● Shape ground beef into 6 oval patties, each about 4 inches long and ¾ inch thick. Sprinkle with salt and pepper.
  Place patties on an unheated rack in a broiler pan. Broil 3 to 4 inches from heat to desired doneness, turning once (allow about 12 minutes total for medium).

12 ½-inch-thick slices French bread, toasted
Easy Dijon Sauce
Ratatouille (see recipe, below)

● Serve burgers on a slice of French bread with Easy Dijon Sauce. Serve with Ratatouille. Makes 6 servings.

Easy Dijon Sauce: In a small bowl stir together ⅓ cup dairy *sour cream,* 1 tablespoon *Dijon-style mustard,* and 1 teaspoon *milk.* Makes about ⅓ cup.

Believe it or not, the burger is part of the classic cuisine you'll find in the bistros of Paris. Their menus offer specialties such as beef patties adorned with tarragon-parsley butter and hamburgers mounded with anchovies and olives.
  Our French-style burger sports a tangy mustard sauce based on the famous French mustard that's flavored with herbs, spices, and white wine.

Ratatouille

½ cup chopped onion
1 clove garlic, minced
1 tablespoon olive *or* cooking oil

● In a large saucepan cook onion and garlic in hot oil till tender but not brown.

2 cups cubed peeled eggplant
2 medium tomatoes, peeled and chopped (1½ cups)
2 small zucchini, halved lengthwise and sliced (1½ cups)
1 large green pepper, chopped (1 cup)
½ teaspoon dried oregano, crushed
¼ teaspoon sugar
⅛ teaspoon pepper
1 bay leaf

● Add eggplant, tomatoes, zucchini, green pepper, oregano, sugar, pepper, and bay leaf. Bring to boiling. Reduce the heat and simmer, uncovered, about 20 minutes or till excess liquid evaporates. Stir often toward end of cooking. Remove bay leaf before serving. Makes 6 servings.

Team up our French-style burger with another French bistro favorite, ratatouille (ra-ta-TWO-ee)—a mixture of eggplant, squash, green pepper, tomatoes, garlic, and olive oil.

Cheers!

Burgers and beer naturally go together, but with the myriad of brews on the market, which beer should you team with your burgers? Before you pop the tab or flip the cap on your next beer, get to know a little bit more about this ancient thirst quencher (beer has been brewed as far back as 6000 B.C.).

● **Lager beer:** Most beers brewed in the U.S. today are lagers. Lager beers characteristically are pale-colored, mellow-tasting, and light-bodied. They range between 3.2 and 4.0 percent alcohol and average about 150 calories per 12 ounces. Lagers are bottom-fermented, which means the yeasts sink to the bottom of the vat during fermentation.

● **Light beer:** American brand "light" beers have fewer calories (70 to 130 per 12 ounces) than lager beers and are made with a reduced amount of malt and grain. The alcohol content is usually somewhat lower than that of regular lager beers, too.
    European brands use the term "light" beer to distinguish their pale lagers from their dark lagers.

● **Ales:** Unlike lagers, ales are fermented at high temperatures by yeasts that float. They are more full-bodied and taste hoppier than lagers, and range in color from pale to deep amber.

● **Porters and Stouts:** These beers are variations of ales. Porters are dark brown, full-bodied, and less hoppy tasting than ales. Well-roasted barley gives the brew a characteristically chocolaty, bittersweet flavor.
    Stout is also flavored and colored by roasted barley. It has a darker color and more intense, bitter hop taste than porter with a dense, almost syrupy body.

● **Bock:** Bock is a German beer that was originally made during the winter months for drinking in the spring, though it's now produced year-round. Dark brown bock beer is generally sweeter than lager, and is full-bodied, with a sharp, strong aroma. The alcohol content may be more than double that of lager beers.

● **Malt liquor:** Malt liquor is another type of lager, but its alcohol content is usually higher. A malt liquor is marked by a darker color, more bitter flavor, and more robust aroma than lager.

How to serve beer
Although many people enjoy their beer ice-cold, low temperatures numb the taste buds. To better appreciate the true aroma and taste of beer, serve it at 45° for lagers and lighter beers, or 50° to 60° for ales, porters, and stouts.

Food and beer
When it comes to choosing a beverage to serve, beer is even more versatile than wine. It's the perfect companion to the hot and spicy dishes of Mexico, China, and India, but is compatible with almost *all* ethnic cuisines.

Pair fuller-bodied, deep-flavored varieties with robust foods, and lighter-flavored beers with more delicate foods such as shellfish. Dark beers complement sausages and smoked pork; about any brew brings out the best in burgers, steaks, and pizzas.

It's all in the pour
To get the most from your beer, pour it straight down the center of a glass. This releases the fresh aroma and flavor of the hops. Quality beers should have lofty heads, usually 1½ to 2 inches high. Be sure the glasses you use are sparkling clean. Even the slightest smudge or speck of dirt on the glass will keep the head from growing.

Store beer right
High temperatures—over 70°F—break down beer's natural ingredients. So your best bet is to keep your favorite brew on the bottom shelf of your refrigerator, where the temperature is between 40° and 50°. Also keep your beer out of the light. Overexposure to light, whether it's indoor lighting or sunlight, damages beer's taste. Most bottled beer comes in protective green or brown bottles to help screen out damaging light, and cardboard packaging helps protect bottles from light, as well as breakage.

Unlike wines, beer doesn't improve with age, and as a result, brewers have strict quality control and stock rotation procedures in an effort to ensure the freshest product possible for the consumer.

Crunchy Oriental Burgers

1 tablespoon soy sauce ½ teaspoon ground ginger 1½ pounds lean ground beef *or* pork	● In a medium mixing bowl combine soy sauce and ginger. Add ground meat and mix well. Shape meat mixture into twelve ¼-inch-thick patties.
½ cup bean sprouts ¼ cup chopped water chestnuts 2 tablespoons sliced green onion	● For stuffing, in a small mixing bowl combine bean sprouts, water chestnuts, and green onion. Place about *2 tablespoons* stuffing mixture atop each of *6* patties. Spread to within ½ inch of edges. Top with the remaining patties. Press the meat around edges to seal well (see tip, below).
6 hamburger buns, split and toasted	● Place patties on an unheated rack in a broiler pan. Broil 3 to 4 inches from the heat about 13 minutes total or till done, turning once. *Or,* grill patties, on an uncovered grill, directly over *medium-hot* coals for 13 to 14 minutes total or till done, turning once. Serve burgers on buns. Makes 6 servings.

To make sure the fillings in this and all other stuffed burgers are piping hot, cook the burgers till they're well-done.

Between Two Patties

You can put almost anything between two meat patties to create stuffed burgers. Just use the recipes on the next few pages or choose your own stuffing and follow these simple steps for great burgers.

Spoon stuffing onto the center of *half* the patties, spreading it to about ½ inch from the edges. (If the stuffing is closer to the edge, it'll leak out while the burgers cook.)

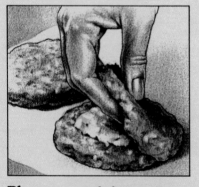

Place a remaining patty on top of each stuffing-topped patty. Then pinch the edges together so they seal well. If necessary, reshape the burgers into even circles.

Greek Stuffed Burgers

1 beaten egg 2 tablespoons dairy sour cream ¼ cup fine dry bread crumbs ¼ teaspoon salt 1 pound ground lamb *or* lean beef	● In a medium mixing bowl combine egg and sour cream. Stir in bread crumbs and salt. Add ground meat and mix well. Shape meat mixture into eight ¼-inch-thick patties.
⅓ cup cream-style cottage cheese, drained 2 tablespoons crumbled feta cheese 2 tablespoons sliced pitted ripe olives	● For stuffing, in a small bowl combine cottage cheese, feta cheese, and ripe olives. Place about *1 tablespoon* stuffing mixture atop each of *4* patties. Spread to within ½ inch of edges. Top with remaining patties. Press meat around edges to seal well (see tip, opposite).
4 hamburger buns, split and toasted 4 tomato slices	● Place patties on an unheated rack in a broiler pan. Broil 3 to 4 inches from the heat about 13 minutes total or till done, turning once. *Or,* grill patties, on an uncovered grill, directly over *medium-hot* coals for 13 to 14 minutes total or till done, turning once. Serve burgers on buns with tomato slices. Serves 4.

Here's the Greek answer to an American cheeseburger. Lamb, feta cheese, and ripe olives transpose an ordinary burger into an irresistible Mediterranean delicacy.

Chutney-Stuffed Turkey Burgers

1 beaten egg ¼ cup fine dry bread crumbs 2 tablespoons thinly sliced green onion 1 pound ground turkey sausage	● In a medium mixing bowl combine egg, bread crumbs, and green onion. Add turkey sausage and mix well. Shape mixture into eight ¼-inch-thick patties.
½ cup shredded carrot ⅓ cup finely chopped chutney 1 tablespoon fine dry bread crumbs	● For stuffing, in a small bowl combine carrot, chutney, and bread crumbs. Place about *1 tablespoon* stuffing mixture atop each of *4* patties. Spread to within ½ inch of edges. Top with remaining patties. Press meat around edges to seal well (see tip, opposite).
4 hamburger buns, split and toasted	● Place patties on an unheated rack in a broiler pan. Broil 3 to 4 inches from the heat about 13 minutes total or till done, turning once. *Or,* grill patties, on an uncovered grill, directly over *medium-hot* coals for 13 to 14 minutes total or till done, turning once. Serve burgers on buns. Makes 4 servings.

Stuff this colorful chutney filling between two pork patties, too.

Prepare burgers as directed at left, *except* substitute 1 pound *ground pork* for the turkey sausage. Then add ½ teaspoon *salt*, ¼ teaspoon ground *sage*, and ⅛ teaspoon *pepper* to the meat mixture.

Feisty Fiesta Burgers

1 beaten egg
¼ teaspoon salt
⅛ teaspoon pepper
    Fiesta Topping
1½ pounds lean ground beef, pork, *or* raw turkey

● In a medium mixing bowl combine egg, salt, pepper, and *3 tablespoons* Fiesta Topping. Add ground meat and mix well. Shape meat mixture into twelve ¼-inch-thick patties.

The mild-mannered appearance of the Fiesta Topping will fool you—it bites back! If there's any left over, use it as a dip for tortilla chips.

¼ cup sliced green onion
¼ cup sliced pitted ripe olives

● For stuffing, in a small bowl combine onion and olives. Place about *1 tablespoon* stuffing mixture atop each of 6 patties. Spread to within ½ inch of edges. Top with remaining patties. Press meat around edges to seal well (*see tip, page 46*).

● Place the patties on an unheated rack in a broiler pan. Broil 3 to 4 inches from the heat about 13 minutes total or till done, turning once. *Or,* grill the patties, on an uncovered grill, directly over *medium-hot* coals for 13 to 14 minutes total or till done, turning once.

6 hamburger buns, split and toasted
    Pickled cherry pepper rings (optional)

● Serve burgers on buns with remaining Fiesta Topping and cherry pepper rings, if desired. Serves 6.

Fiesta Topping: In a blender container or food processor bowl combine 1 medium *avocado,* seeded, peeled, and cut up; ⅓ cup plain *yogurt;* ⅓ cup *mayonnaise or salad dressing;* 1 or 2 canned *jalapeño peppers,* drained, seeded, and coarsely chopped (1 tablespoon); ¼ teaspoon *salt;* dash *pepper;* and 1 small clove *garlic,* minced. Cover and blend or process till very smooth. Makes about 1½ cups.

Pesto Burgers

1 beaten egg 2 tablespoons dairy sour cream ⅓ cup fine dry bread crumbs 1½ pounds lamb, lean ground beef, *or* pork	● In a medium mixing bowl combine egg and sour cream. Stir in bread crumbs. Add ground meat and mix well. Shape the meat mixture into twelve ¼-inch-thick patties.
Pesto Stuffing (see recipe, right)	● Place about *1 tablespoon* Pesto Stuffing atop each of *6* patties. Spread to within ½ inch of edges. Top with remaining patties. Press meat around edges to seal well (see tip, page 46).
6 lettuce leaves 6 hamburger buns, split and toasted 6 tomato slices	● Place patties on an unheated rack in a broiler pan. Broil 3 to 4 inches from the heat about 13 minutes total or till done, turning once. *Or,* grill patties, on an uncovered grill, directly over *medium-hot* coals for 13 to 14 minutes total or till done, turning once. Serve burgers on lettuce-lined buns with tomato slices. Makes 6 servings.

Pesto Stuffing: Place 3 tablespoons *cooking oil* in a blender container. Add 2 cups lightly packed snipped *parsley;* 2 tablespoons *walnuts;* 1 teaspoon dried *basil,* crushed; and 1 clove *garlic,* quartered. Cover and blend till nearly smooth. Stir in ¼ cup grated *Parmesan cheese.* Makes ⅔ cup.

Mushroom Burgers

1 beaten egg 2 tablespoons prepared horseradish ¼ cup fine dry bread crumbs 1 tablespoon snipped parsley *or* 1 teaspoon dried parsley flakes ½ teaspoon dried basil, crushed 1 pound lean ground beef, lamb, *or* raw turkey 1 4-ounce can mushroom stems and pieces, drained and chopped	● In a medium mixing bowl combine egg and horseradish. Stir in bread crumbs, parsley, and basil. Add ground meat and mix well. Shape meat mixture into eight ¼-inch-thick patties. Place about ¼ of the mushrooms atop each of *4* patties. Spread to within ½ inch of edges. Top with remaining patties. Press meat around edges to seal well (see tip, page 46).
4 slices mozzarella cheese 4 lettuce leaves 4 hamburger buns, split and toasted	● Place patties on an unheated rack in a broiler pan. Broil 3 to 4 inches from the heat about 13 minutes total or till done, turning once. *Or,* grill patties, on an uncovered grill, directly over *medium-hot* coals for 13 to 14 minutes total or till done, turning once. Top burgers with cheese. Heat just till cheese melts. Serve on lettuce-lined buns. Makes 4 servings.

Meat takes a big chunk out of your grocery budget, so when you're freezing the meat, protect your investment by properly wrapping it.

Wrap tightly to press out air pockets. Use freezer paper or wrap 1½ times longer than needed to go around the meat. Place meat in the center of coated side of the paper. Bring the sides of the paper together at top. Fold the edges down in a series of locked folds. Crease the ends of the paper into points. Secure both ends of the paper on top of the meat with freezer tape. Label the package with its contents and the date.

Caper Burgers

1 beaten egg
2 tablespoons plain yogurt
¼ cup fine dry bread crumbs
Dash pepper
1 pound lean ground beef *or* pork

● In a medium mixing bowl combine egg and yogurt. Stir in bread crumbs and pepper. Add ground meat and mix well. Shape the meat mixture into eight ¼-inch-thick patties.

Capers add a lively pickled flavor to just about anything, including these stuffed burgers. The tiny, olive green pods are flower buds picked before the petals can open and then soaked in vinegar or salt.

3 tablespoons capers
1 tablespoon brown mustard

● For stuffing, mix capers and mustard. Place about *1 tablespoon* stuffing mixture atop each of *4* patties. Spread to within ½ inch of edges. Top with remaining patties. Press meat around edges to seal well (see tip, page 46).

2 slices Swiss cheese
4 spinach leaves
4 kaiser rolls, split and toasted

● Place patties on an unheated rack in a broiler pan. Broil 3 to 4 inches from the heat about 13 minutes total till done, turning once. *Or,* grill patties, on an uncovered grill, directly over *medium-hot* coals for 13 to 14 minutes total, turning once. Top burgers with cheese. Heat just till cheese melts. Serve burgers on spinach-lined kaiser rolls. Serves 4.

Blue Cheese Burgers

1 beaten egg
1 tablespoon Worcestershire sauce
⅓ cup fine dry rye bread crumbs
1 teaspoon prepared mustard
⅛ teaspoon pepper
Dash garlic powder
1½ pounds lean ground beef

● In a medium mixing bowl combine egg and Worcestershire sauce. Stir in rye bread crumbs, mustard, pepper, and garlic powder. Add ground beef and mix well. Shape the meat mixture into twelve ¼-inch-thick patties.

Deciphering the labels on ground beef packages can be confusing. Often packages are labeled ground round, ground sirloin, or ground chuck (ground round being the most lean, followed by sirloin, and then chuck).
   When choosing meat for burgers, consider how you're going to cook them. For broiled burgers, consider buying ground chuck (the fat drains away during broiling). For barbecued burgers, choose leaner meat, so fat doesn't drip onto hot coals and cause flare-ups.

¾ cup crumbled blue cheese

● Place about *2 tablespoons* blue cheese atop each of *6* patties. Spread to within ½ inch of edges. Top with remaining patties. Press meat around edges to seal well (see tip, page 46).

6 hamburger buns, split and toasted
Alfalfa sprouts

● Place patties on a rack in an unheated broiler pan. Broil 3 to 4 inches from the heat about 13 minutes total or till done, turning once. *Or,* grill patties, on an uncovered grill, directly over *medium-hot* coals for 13 to 14 minutes total or till done, turning once. Serve burgers on buns with alfalfa sprouts. Serves 6.

Use a spoon to spread the colorful vegetable stuffing over the smaller circle of meat. Carefully place the larger circle of meat on top of the stuffing. Peel off the waxed paper.

Use your fingers to pinch the edges of the meat together so they seal. Reshape the burger into an even circle, if necessary.

Big Vegetable-Stuffed Burger

1 cup shredded potato
   (about 1 medium)
½ cup shredded carrot
½ cup shredded zucchini
¼ cup chopped onion
2 tablespoons butter *or*
   margarine
1 beaten egg
1 tablespoon fine dry bread
   crumbs
¼ teaspoon dried marjoram,
   crushed

● For stuffing, in a 10-inch skillet cook potato, carrot, zucchini, and onion, covered, in butter or margarine till vegetables are tender, stirring occasionally.
   In a medium mixing bowl combine cooked vegetables, egg, bread crumbs, and marjoram.

Dig right in! The best way to combine burger mixtures is with your hands. Use a fork to stir together the egg, liquid, bread crumbs, and seasoning. After the meat is added, blend it all together with your hands so the ingredients get evenly distributed.

2 beaten eggs
¼ cup milk
¼ cup fine dry bread crumbs
3 tablespoons snipped
   parsley
½ teaspoon salt
   Dash pepper
2 pounds lean ground beef,
   pork, lamb, *or*
   raw turkey

● In a medium mixing bowl combine eggs and milk. Stir in bread crumbs, parsley, salt, and pepper. Add ground meat and mix well.
   In a 9x9x2-inch baking pan, pat *half* of the meat mixture into a 7-inch circle. (If grilling, pat out meat mixture on a sheet of waxed paper.) On a sheet of waxed paper pat the remaining meat mixture into an 8-inch circle.
   Spread stuffing mixture on the smaller circle to within ½ inch of edges. Invert the 8-inch circle atop. Peel off waxed paper. Press meat around edges to seal well (see photo, left).

● Bake in a 350° oven for 60 to 70 minutes or till well-done, spooning off fat as it accumulates. *Or,* in a covered grill arrange preheated coals around a drip pan. Test for *medium* heat above pan. (Brush cold grill rack with cooking oil if using turkey.) Invert burger onto grill rack over drip pan but not over coals. Peel off waxed paper. Lower grill hood. Grill for 60 minutes or till well-done.

¼ cup catsup
2 tablespoons brown sugar
1 teaspoon dry mustard
   Green onion brushes
   (optional)
   Carrot curls (optional)

● Meanwhile, for glaze, in a small bowl combine catsup, brown sugar, and mustard. Spread glaze over burger during the last 10 minutes of baking or grilling. Garnish with onion brushes and carrot curls, if desired. Makes 8 servings.

Jumbo Fruit And Rice Burger

⅔ cup apple cider *or* apple juice
⅓ cup long grain rice
1 tablespoon butter *or* margarine
¼ teaspoon salt
⅛ teaspoon ground cinnamon
½ cup chopped mixed dried fruits
2 tablespoons snipped parsley

● For stuffing, in a small saucepan combine cider or juice, rice, butter or margarine, salt, and cinnamon. Bring to boiling. Reduce heat and simmer for 10 minutes. Stir in dried fruits and parsley. Cook, covered, for 5 minutes more.

Curry Sauce: In a small saucepan cook ½ cup chopped *onion*, 2 to 3 teaspoons *curry powder*, and 1 clove *garlic*, minced, in 2 tablespoons *butter or margarine* till tender. Stir in 2 tablespoons all-purpose *flour*. Add 1 cup *apple cider or apple juice* all at once. Cook and stir till thickened and bubbly, then cook and stir for 1 minute more. Makes about 1 cup.

2 beaten eggs
¼ cup apple cider *or* apple juice
⅓ cup fine dry bread crumbs
2 pounds lean ground beef, lamb, *or* raw turkey

● In a medium mixing bowl combine eggs and cider or juice. Stir in bread crumbs. Add ground meat and mix well.
In a 9x9x2-inch baking pan, pat *half* of the meat mixture into a 7-inch circle. (If grilling, pat out meat mixture on a sheet of waxed paper.) On a sheet of waxed paper pat the remaining meat mixture into an 8-inch circle.
Spread stuffing mixture on the smaller circle to within ½ inch of edges. Invert the 8-inch circle atop. Peel off waxed paper. Press meat around edges to seal well (see photos, page 52).

● Bake in a 350° oven for 60 to 70 minutes or till well-done, spooning off fat as it accumulates. *Or,* in a covered grill arrange preheated coals around a drip pan. Test for *medium* heat above pan. (Brush the cold grill rack with cooking oil if using turkey.) Invert burger onto grill rack over drip pan but not over coals. Peel off waxed paper. Lower the grill hood. Grill for 60 minutes or till well-done.

Curry Sauce (see recipe, right)
3 tablespoons chopped peanuts

● Drizzle some of the Curry Sauce over burger. Sprinkle with chopped peanuts. Pass remaining sauce. Makes 8 servings.

Florentine-Stuffed Burger

½ of a 10-ounce package
  frozen chopped spinach
¼ cup sliced green onion
1 4-ounce can mushroom
  stems and pieces,
  drained and chopped
⅓ cup grated Parmesan
  cheese

● For stuffing, cook spinach and onion according to package directions for spinach, then drain well. Stir in mushrooms and Parmesan cheese.

Use a foil drip pan to catch juices and fat that cook out of grilled meat.
  Tear off a piece of 18-inch-wide *heavy* foil twice the length of your grill. Fold it in half for a double thickness. Turn the edges up 1½ inches.

2 pounds lean ground beef
  or pork
  Garlic salt
  Pepper

● In a 9x9x2-inch baking pan, pat *half* of the meat into a 7-inch circle. (If grilling, pat out meat on a sheet of waxed paper.) On a sheet of waxed paper pat the remaining meat into an 8-inch circle. Sprinkle meat with garlic salt and pepper.
  Spread stuffing mixture on the smaller circle to within ½ inch of edges. Invert the 8-inch circle atop. Peel off waxed paper. Press meat around edges to seal well (see photos, page 52).

● Bake in a 350° oven for 60 to 70 minutes or till well-done, spooning off fat as it accumulates. *Or,* in a covered grill arrange preheated coals around a drip pan (see photos, right). Test for *medium* heat above pan. Invert burger onto grill rack over drip pan but not over coals. Peel off waxed paper. Lower grill hood. Grill about 60 minutes or till well-done.

Miter the corners by pressing the tips of the corners together and folding them to the side.

Sour Cream Sauce

● Drizzle some of the Sour Cream Sauce over burger. Pass remaining sauce. Makes 8 servings.

Sour Cream Sauce: Combine ½ cup dairy *sour cream* and 1 tablespoon all-purpose *flour;* set aside. In a small saucepan combine 3 tablespoons *water;* 2 tablespoons sliced *green onion;* 2 tablespoons *dry white wine;* and ¼ teaspoon dried *tarragon,* crushed. Bring to boiling. Cook, uncovered, for 1 minute. Stir sour cream mixture into wine mixture. Cook and stir till thickened and bubbly. Cook and stir for 1 minute more. Makes about 1 cup.

Giant Tex-Mex Burger

1 beaten egg
¼ cup salsa
½ cup canned refried beans
¼ cup fine dry bread crumbs
¼ cup finely chopped onion
2 to 3 tablespoons canned jalapeño peppers, drained, seeded, and chopped
2 teaspoons chili powder
¼ teaspoon salt
2 pounds lean ground beef *or* pork
¼ cup shredded cheddar cheese (1 ounce)
Tortilla chips
Dairy sour cream
Pickled cherry peppers (optional)

● Combine egg and salsa. Stir in beans, bread crumbs, onion, peppers, chili powder, and salt. Add meat; mix well.

In a 9x9x2-inch baking pan, pat meat mixture into a 7-inch round loaf. (If grilling, pat out meat mixture on a sheet of waxed paper.) Bake in a 350° oven for 60 to 70 minutes or till well-done, spooning off fat as it accumulates. *Or,* in a covered grill, arrange preheated coals around a drip pan. Test for *medium* heat above pan. Invert burger onto grill rack over the drip pan but not over coals. Peel off waxed paper. Lower the grill hood. Grill for 60 minutes or till well-done. Sprinkle with cheese during the last 5 minutes of baking or grilling.

Serve on a platter surrounded with chips. Top with sour cream. Garnish with pickled peppers, if desired. Serves 8.

Extra salsa and a little green onion for topping will make this giant burger taste like a first cousin to nachos.

Big Bacon-Stuffed Burger

5 slices bacon
¼ cup finely chopped green pepper
¼ cup chopped onion
1 4-ounce can chopped mushrooms, drained

● For stuffing, in a 10-inch skillet cook bacon till crisp. Drain bacon, reserving 1 tablespoon drippings. Crumble bacon and reserve *2 tablespoons* for garnish.

In the skillet cook green pepper and onion in reserved drippings till tender but not brown. Stir in mushrooms and remaining bacon.

When buying bacon, remember to compare prices by cost per pound not cost per package. Divide the price of a 16-ounce package by four and the price of a 12-ounce package by three. Then compare.

1 beaten egg
3 tablespoons milk
1 tablespoon Worcestershire sauce
½ cup herb-seasoned stuffing mix, slightly crushed
2 tablespoons snipped parsley
2 pounds lean ground beef, pork, *or* raw turkey

● In a medium mixing bowl combine egg, milk, and Worcestershire sauce. Stir in stuffing mix and parsley. Add ground meat and mix well.

In a 9x9x2-inch baking pan, pat *half* of the meat mixture into a 7-inch circle. (If grilling, pat out *half* of the meat mixture on a sheet of waxed paper.) On a sheet of waxed paper pat the remaining meat mixture into an 8-inch circle.

Spread stuffing mixture on smaller circle to within ½ inch of edges. Invert 8-inch circle atop. Peel off waxed paper. Press meat around edges to seal well (see photos, page 52).

● Bake in a 350° oven for 60 to 70 minutes or till well-done, spooning off fat as it accumulates. *Or,* in a covered grill, arrange preheated coals around a drip pan. Test for *medium* heat above pan. (Brush cold grill rack with cooking oil if using turkey.) Invert burger onto grill rack over drip pan but not over coals. Peel off waxed paper. Lower grill hood. Grill for 60 minutes or till well-done.

Beer-Cheese Sauce

● To serve, drizzle some of the Beer-Cheese Sauce over burger. Sprinkle with reserved crumbled bacon. Pass remaining sauce. Makes 8 servings.

Beer-Cheese Sauce: In a small bowl toss together ¾ cup shredded *American cheese* (3 ounces), 4 teaspoons *all-purpose flour*, and ½ teaspoon *dry mustard.* In a small saucepan heat ⅓ cup *beer* till almost boiling. Add cheese mixture and a few dashes *bottled hot pepper sauce.* Cook and stir till cheese is melted. Add ¼ cup *milk*, stirring till smooth. Cook till heated through. Makes ¾ cup sauce.

Pinwheel Burger Slices

10 slices bacon
½ cup shredded carrot
¼ cup sliced green onion
2 tablespoons finely
    chopped celery
1 4-ounce can mushroom
    stems and pieces,
    drained and chopped

● Partially cook bacon in a large skillet (see directions, right). Drain bacon on paper towels, reserving about 1 tablespoon drippings in skillet.

For the filling, cook carrot, onion, and celery in reserved drippings till tender but not brown. Stir mushrooms into cooked vegetables.

1 beaten egg
2 tablespoons milk
¼ cup fine dry bread crumbs
2 tablespoons grated
    Parmesan cheese
1 pound lean ground beef,
    or pork

● In a medium mixing bowl combine egg and milk. Stir in bread crumbs and Parmesan cheese. Add the ground meat and mix well.

Pat meat mixture into a 7½-inch square. Spread filling evenly over meat. Roll up jelly-roll style. Carefully cut meat roll into five 1½-inch-thick slices. Wrap *2* strips of partially cooked bacon around *each* meat slice. Secure bacon strips with wooden toothpicks.

● Place meat slices on an unheated rack in a broiler pan. Broil 4 inches from the heat to desired doneness, turning once (allow about 11 minutes total for medium and about 14 minutes total for well-done). (Always cook pork till well-done.) Remove toothpicks before serving. Makes 5 servings.

The bacon around these slices finishes cooking under the broiler, so just partially cook it before you wrap it around the meat.

The bacon will cook more evenly if you don't crowd it. Fry it *half* at a time in a 10- or 12-inch skillet over medium heat for 3 to 4 minutes or till it's limp but not brown.

4 Served these dressed-up slices with a salad and vegetable for an elegant, yet inexpensive, meal.

1 Spread the vegetable filling over the meat, pressing it in slightly. Roll up the meat square jelly-roll style.

2 Using a sharp knife, gently cut the meat roll into five slices, making each slice about 1½ inches thick.

3 Wrap two partially cooked bacon slices around each meat slice. Use wooden toothpicks to hold the bacon in place.

Taco Turnovers

1 4-ounce can diced green chili peppers, drained
¼ cup jalapeño bean dip
¼ teaspoon salt
1½ pounds lean ground beef
3 ounces Monterey Jack cheese with jalapeño peppers, thinly sliced

● In a medium mixing bowl combine chili peppers, bean dip, and salt. Add ground beef and mix well.

On waxed paper, pat meat mixture into a 12x8-inch rectangle. Cut rectangle into six 4-inch squares. Place a little cheese diagonally atop half of *each* square, tearing as necessary to fit. Fold *each* meat square in half diagonally over cheese to form a triangle (see photo, right). Press meat around edges to seal.

Place the meat triangles on an unheated rack in a broiler pan. Broil 3 to 4 inches from the heat to desired doneness, turning once (allow about 10 minutes total for medium).

Cover a *diagonal* half of each meat square with cheese, tearing the cheese to fit as you go. Lightly press the cheese pieces into the meat.

Using the waxed paper as a lifter, carefully fold each meat square over the cheese, forming a triangle.

6 cups shredded lettuce
3 cups corn chips
Dairy sour cream
Chopped tomato
Taco sauce (optional)

● To serve, arrange *1 cup* lettuce on *each* of 6 plates, then top with ½ *cup* corn chips. Place *1* cooked turnover atop corn chips. Top with sour cream and chopped tomato.

Serve with taco sauce, if desired. Makes 6 servings.

Welsh Rarebit Burgers

1 pound lean ground beef, pork, *or* lamb

● Shape meat into four ¾-inch-thick patties. Place patties on an unheated rack in a broiler pan. Broil 3 to 4 inches from heat to desired doneness, turning once (allow about 12 minutes total for medium and 14 minutes total for well-done). (Always cook pork till well-done.)

Ever heard of Welsh Rabbit? It's a culinary joke that legend says began when Welsh housewives were forced to serve cheese to guests because their hunter husbands failed to bag a rabbit. Cooks probably began calling it rarebit because it sounded more refined.

¾ cup shredded American cheese (3 ounces)
¾ cup shredded cheddar cheese (3 ounces)
1½ teaspoons all-purpose flour
1 teaspoon dry mustard
¾ cup beer
1 teaspoon Worcestershire sauce
Dash bottled hot pepper sauce
1 beaten egg

● Meanwhile, for sauce, toss together the cheeses, flour, and dry mustard. In a heavy saucepan combine cheese mixture, beer, Worcestershire sauce, and hot pepper sauce. Cook and stir over medium heat till thickened and bubbly and cheese melts. Slowly stir about *half* of the hot mixture into beaten egg. Return all to pan. Cook and stir over low heat till mixture thickens and starts to bubble. *Do not boil.*

2 English muffins, split and toasted
Crumbled cooked bacon (optional)

● Serve burgers on English muffin halves with sauce. Sprinkle with crumbled bacon, if desired. Serve immediately. Makes 4 servings.

Fish Patties Vera Cruz

1 **pound fresh *or* frozen fish fillets** **Water** **Salt**	● Thaw fish, if frozen. Place a greased rack in a large skillet with a tight-fitting lid. Add water till it almost reaches rack. Bring water to boiling. Sprinkle fish with salt. Place fish on rack. Cover pan and steam till fish flakes easily when tested with a fork (allow about 4 minutes per ½-inch thickness). Lift out rack. Carefully remove fish from rack and cool. Flake fish and set aside (see photo, page 21). You should have 2 cups.
2 **beaten eggs** ⅓ **cup fine dry bread crumbs** 2 **tablespoons snipped parsley** ½ **teaspoon grated gingerroot** 1⅓ **cups cooked rice** ¼ **cup all-purpose flour**	● In a medium mixing bowl combine eggs, bread crumbs, parsley, and gingerroot. Stir in rice. Add flaked fish and mix well. Cover and chill for 1 hour for easier handling. Shape mixture into six ¾-inch-thick patties. Coat patties with flour.
2 **tablespoons cooking oil *or* shortening**	● In a 12-inch skillet cook patties in hot oil or shortening over medium-low heat about 6 minutes on each side or till golden brown.
½ **cup chopped onion** 1 **clove garlic, minced** 1 **tablespoon cooking oil** 1 **10-ounce can tomatoes and green chili peppers** 2 **tablespoons dry white wine** **Dash to ⅛ teaspoon ground red pepper** **Dash ground cinnamon** 2 **tablespoons sliced pimiento-stuffed olives**	● Meanwhile, for sauce, in a small saucepan cook onion and garlic in hot oil till tender but not brown. Stir in *undrained* tomatoes and green chili peppers, wine, red pepper, and cinnamon. Bring mixture to boiling. Boil gently, uncovered, about 10 minutes or till slightly thickened. Stir in olives.
Parsley sprigs (optional)	● Serve patties on a platter with sauce. Garnish with parsley, if desired. Serves 6.

Our south-of-the-border amigos know how to make a mean sauce! These fish patties are smothered with a traditional Mexican Vera Cruz sauce that's full of tomatoes, garlic, onion, chili peppers, red pepper, and a hint of cinnamon.

Easy Burgers Wellington

1	**tablespoon dry red wine**
1	**pound lean ground beef** **or lamb**
	Garlic salt

● In a mixing bowl combine wine and ground meat. Mix well. Shape meat mixture into four ¾-inch-thick patties.

Preheat a heavy 10-inch skillet over high heat till hot. Sprinkle surface of skillet lightly with garlic salt. Add patties. Reduce heat to medium-low. Cook to desired doneness, turning once, spooning off fat as it accumulates (allow about 11 minutes total for medium). Drain burgers on a plate lined with a double thickness of paper towels. Drain fat from skillet.

1	**cup finely chopped fresh mushrooms (4 ounces)**
¼	**cup sliced green onion**
1	**tablespoon butter or margarine**
1	**tablespoon dry red wine**

● In the skillet cook mushrooms and green onion in butter or margarine about 3 minutes or till tender. Stir in wine and ¼ teaspoon *pepper*. Cook for 1 to 2 minutes more or till liquid is evaporated. Remove from the heat.

1	**package (8) refrigerated crescent rolls**
	Milk

● Meanwhile, unroll crescent rolls. Seal perforations to form 4 rectangles. On lightly floured surface, roll each rectangle to a 7-inch square. Cut corners off the pastry squares and set aside (see photo, right). Spoon about ¼ of the mushroom mixture in the center of *each* square. Place a burger atop the mushroom mixture on each square. Draw pastry up around the burger (see photo, right). Pinch edges to seal. Place seam side down in a greased shallow baking pan.

Make cutouts from reserved pastry (see photo, right). Brush top and sides of pastry with milk. Place cutouts on meat bundles. Bake in a 400° oven for 10 to 12 minutes or till golden brown. Makes 4 servings.

Roll pastry rectangles into 7-inch squares. Cut off the corners of each square.

Pull the pastry up and around the burger, trimming off any excess dough. Pinch the edges to seal well.

Using small cookie or hors d'oeuvres cutters, cut out different designs for the tops of the meat bundles. Use the reserved pastry corners and any excess dough you trimmed off.

Ham Pastries

2 beaten eggs
2 tablespoons milk
1 cup finely chopped celery
1 cup shredded carrot
½ cup fine dry bread crumbs
½ cup finely chopped onion
1 teaspoon prepared
   horseradish
1 teaspoon soy sauce
¼ teaspoon pepper
1 pound ground fully
   cooked ham

● In a medium mixing bowl combine eggs and milk. Stir in celery, carrot, bread crumbs, onion, horseradish, soy sauce, and pepper. Add the ground ham and mix well.
   Shape mixture into six ¾-inch-thick patties. Place patties in a well-greased shallow baking pan.

Shape the ham mixture into patties, using about ¾ cup of the mixture for each. Place the rolled-out pastry shells over the patties, tucking them under slightly.

6 frozen patty shells,
   thawed
   Milk

● On a lightly floured surface, roll each patty shell into a 5-inch circle. Drape *1* circle over *each* ham patty (see photo, right). Brush lightly with milk. Preheat oven to 450°.
   Place pastries in oven. Reduce oven to 400°. Bake for 25 to 30 minutes or till golden brown. Serve immediately. Makes 6 servings.

Hamburgers Au Poivre

2 to 4 teaspoons whole
   black pepper
1 pound lean ground beef
   Salt

● Coarsely crack black pepper. Shape beef into four ¾-inch-thick patties. Lightly press cracked pepper into *both* sides of *each* patty (see photo, right).
   Preheat a heavy 10-inch skillet over high heat till hot. Sprinkle surface lightly with salt. Add patties. Reduce the heat to medium-low. Cook to desired doneness, turning once, spooning off fat as it accumulates (allow about 11 minutes total for medium). Drain patties and keep warm. Drain fat from skillet.

Use a mortar and pestle or a pepper mill to make quick work of cracking the whole black pepper. Lightly press half of the pepper into one side of the patties, then turn and press the remaining pepper into the other side.

¼ cup sliced green onion
1 small clove garlic, minced
1 tablespoon butter *or*
   margarine
⅓ cup water
1 teaspoon instant beef
   bouillon granules
3 tablespoons brandy

● In the skillet cook onion and garlic in butter or margarine till tender but not brown. Stir in water and bouillon granules. Bring to boiling, then boil for 1 minute. Stir in brandy and cook for 1 minute more. Pour over burgers. Makes 4 servings.

Soufflé-Topped Pork Burgers

1 beaten egg 2 tablespoons milk ¼ cup fine dry bread crumbs ¼ teaspoon dried thyme, crushed ¼ teaspoon pepper ½ pound ground fully cooked ham ½ pound ground pork	● In a medium mixing bowl combine egg and milk. Stir in bread crumbs, thyme, and pepper. Add ground ham and ground pork and mix well. Shape meat mixture into four ¾-inch-thick patties. Place patties on an unheated rack in a broiler pan. Broil 3 to 4 inches from the heat about 14 minutes total or till well-done, turning once. Keep warm.
⅓ cup mayonnaise *or* salad dressing ¼ cup shredded cheddar *or* Swiss cheese 2 tablespoons grated Parmesan cheese ½ teaspoon finely shredded lemon peel 1 egg white ⅛ teaspoon cream of tartar	● In a small bowl combine mayonnaise or salad dressing, cheddar or Swiss cheese, Parmesan cheese, and lemon peel. In a small mixer bowl use a rotary beater to beat egg white and cream of tartar till stiff peaks form (tips stand straight). Fold beaten egg white into mayonnaise mixture. Carefully spoon about ¼ of the egg white mixture atop *each* cooked burger. Continue broiling for 2 to 3 minutes more or till egg white mixture is soft-set and golden brown (see photo, below).
Shredded lettuce Radish slices (optional)	● Serve burgers on shredded lettuce with radish slices, if desired. Serves 4.

The soufflé on these burgers is really a mixture of mayonnaise, cheese, and fluffy egg white.

Spoon a little bit of the egg white topping on each burger. Put the burgers back under the broiler till the topping becomes a light golden brown and is soft-set.

Beer-Onion Buns

1 **16-ounce package hot roll mix**
¼ **cup grated Parmesan cheese**
1 **cup finely chopped onion**
2 **tablespoons butter or margarine**
1¼ **cups beer**

● In a large mixing bowl combine flour and yeast from hot roll mix and Parmesan cheese. Set aside.

In a small saucepan cook onion in butter or margarine till tender but not brown. Remove *half* of the cooked onion from the pan and set aside.

Add beer to saucepan and heat just till warm (115° to 120°). Remove from the heat. Stir beer mixture into flour-cheese mixture, stirring till well combined.

● Turn out onto a lightly floured surface (see illustrations, page 68). Knead for 2 to 3 minutes. (If dough seems sticky, sprinkle with a little all-purpose flour.) Shape into a ball. Place in a lightly greased bowl. Turn dough once to grease the surface. Cover and let the dough rise in a warm place till double (30 to 45 minutes).

Punch dough down. Cover and let rest for 10 minutes. Divide into 8 portions. Shape each into an even circle, folding edges under. Press flat between your hands. Place on a greased baking sheet. Press into 3-inch circles. Cover and let rise till nearly double (20 to 30 minutes). Brush reserved onion over tops of buns.

Bake in a 375° oven for 12 to 15 minutes. Remove from sheet. Cool on wire racks. Makes 8 buns.

With homemade buns this easy to make and so delicious, you may forget about store-bought buns forever!

Quick-Rise Whole Wheat Buns *(see recipe, page 69)*, **Cornmeal-Mustard Buns** *(see recipe, page 70)*, **Swiss-Rye Buns** *(see recipe, page 71)*, **and Beer-Onion Buns.**

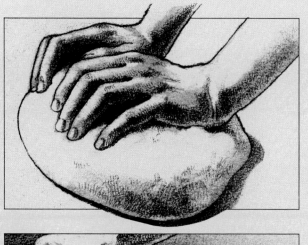
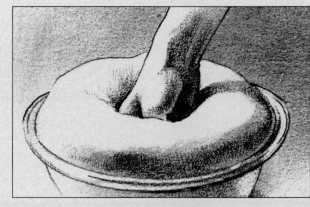
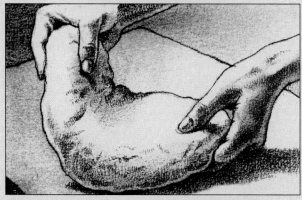
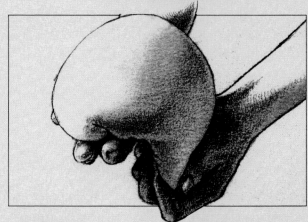

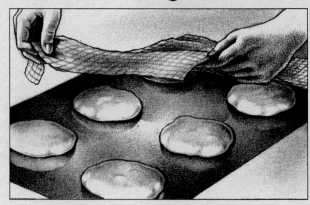

Making Buns

1 To knead, place the dough on a lightly floured surface or a well-floured pastry cloth. Fold the dough over and push it down with the heels of your hands, curving your fingers over the dough.

2 Give the dough a quarter-turn, then fold it over and push it down again. Continue kneading, adding enough of the remaining flour to prevent stickiness, till the dough is smooth and elastic.

3 The dough is doubled and ready to shape when you can press two fingers ½ inch into the dough and the indentations remain.

4 To punch the dough down, push your fist into the center of the dough. Pull the edges of the dough to the center. Turn the dough over and place it on a lightly floured surface to rest.

5 Divide dough into 12 portions. Shape each by folding the edges under to make even circles.

6 Press each circle flat between your hands. Place on greased baking sheets and press into 3½-inch circles. Cover with a cloth and let rise till nearly double.

Fast-Rise Whole Wheat Buns

Pictured on pages 66–67.

2¾ to 3¼ cups all-purpose flour
2 packages active dry yeast
1⅔ cups milk
⅓ cup honey
2 tablespoons butter *or* margarine
½ teaspoon salt
1 egg
2½ cups whole wheat flour

● In a large mixer bowl combine *2 cups* of the all-purpose flour and yeast.

In a medium saucepan heat milk, honey, butter or margarine, and salt just till warm (115° to 120°) and butter is almost melted, stirring constantly. Add to flour mixture along with egg.

Beat with electric mixer on low speed for ½ minute, scraping sides of bowl constantly. Beat for 3 minutes on high speed. Stir in whole wheat flour and as much of the remaining all-purpose flour as you can mix in with a spoon.

Test Kitchen Tip: To save time, use the quick method for proofing bread: Place the covered dough in a warm oven to rise. This method, noted in the recipe at left, works well for these whole wheat buns and for the Swiss-Rye Buns and Cornmeal-Mustard Buns (pages 70 and 71).

● Turn out onto a lightly floured surface (see illustrations, left). Knead in enough of the remaining all-purpose flour to make a moderately stiff dough that is smooth and elastic (6 to 8 minutes total). Shape dough into a ball. Place dough in a lightly greased bowl. Turn once to grease surface.

Turn the oven on to 200° for *1 minute* for an electric oven or *2 minutes* for gas. Turn the oven off. *Quickly* place covered dough in the warm oven till double (about 30 minutes).

● Punch dough down. Cover and let rest for 10 minutes. Divide into 12 portions. Shape each into an even circle, folding edges under. Press flat between hands. Place onto 2 greased baking sheets. Press into 3-inch circles.

Turn the oven on to 200° for *1 minute* for an electric oven or *2 minutes* for gas. Turn the oven off. *Quickly* place covered dough in warm oven till nearly double (about 30 minutes). Remove from the oven. Preheat the oven to 375°.

1 beaten egg white
1 tablespoon water
Toasted wheat germ
Sesame seed

● Combine egg white and water. Brush tops of buns with egg white-water mixture. Sprinkle with wheat germ or sesame seed. If desired, with a sharp knife make 5 slashes on tops of buns from center to outside edges, forming a star-shape design. Bake in 375° oven for 15 to 20 minutes. Remove from sheets. Cool on wire racks. Makes 12 buns.

Cornmeal-Mustard Buns

Pictured on pages 66–67.

3¾ to 4¼ cups all-purpose
    flour
 ½ cup yellow cornmeal
  1 package active dry yeast
1½ cups milk
  1 tablespoon sugar
  1 tablespoon shortening
 ¼ teaspoon salt
  1 egg
  3 tablespoons prepared
    mustard

● In a large mixer bowl combine *1½ cups* of the flour, cornmeal, and yeast.
  In a small saucepan heat milk, sugar, shortening, and salt just till warm (115° to 120°) and shortening is almost melted, stirring constantly. Add to flour mixture along with egg and mustard.
  Beat with electric mixer on low speed for ½ minute, scraping sides of bowl constantly. Beat for 3 minutes on high speed. Stir in as much of the remaining flour as you can mix in with a spoon.

● Turn out onto a lightly floured surface (see illustrations, page 68). Knead in enough of the remaining flour to make a moderately stiff dough that is smooth and elastic (6 to 8 minutes total). Shape into a ball. Place in a lightly greased bowl. Turn dough once to grease the surface. Cover and let rise in a warm place till double (about 1 hour).

● Punch dough down. Cover and let rest for 10 minutes. Divide into 12 portions. Shape each into an even circle, folding edges under. Press flat between hands. Place on 2 greased baking sheets. Press into 3-inch circles. Cover and let rise till nearly double (about 45 minutes).

1 beaten egg white
1 tablespoon water

● Combine egg white and water. Brush tops of buns with egg white and water mixture. If desired, with a sharp knife make 5 slashes on the tops of buns from center to outside edges, forming a star-shape design. Bake in a 375° oven for 15 to 20 minutes. Remove from sheets. Cool on wire racks. Makes 12 buns.

Knock off one-third to one-half of the rising time by using quick-rising dry yeast.

Swiss-Rye Buns

Pictured on pages 66–67.

3¼ to 3¾ cups all-purpose
        flour
   2 packages active dry yeast
   2 tablespoons caraway seed
   2 cups milk
   ⅓ cup packed brown sugar
   ¼ cup cooking oil
   ¼ teaspoon salt
   2 eggs
   1 cup shredded Swiss *or*
        cheddar cheese
   3 cups rye flour

● In a large mixer bowl combine *2½ cups* of the all-purpose flour, yeast, and caraway seed.

In a medium saucepan heat milk, brown sugar, oil, and salt just till warm (115° to 120°). Add to flour mixture along with eggs and cheese.

Beat with electric mixer on low speed for ½ minute, scraping sides of bowl constantly. Beat for 3 minutes on high speed. Stir in rye flour and as much of the remaining all-purpose flour as you can mix in with a spoon.

Spread an extra-thick layer of Crunchy Mustard (page 73) on one of these great-tasting buns, then fill with a grilled bratwurst—yum, yum, yum! (For frankfurter buns, shape the dough into rolls about 5½ inches long.)

● Turn out onto a lightly floured surface (see illustrations, page 68). Knead in enough of the remaining all-purpose flour to make a moderately stiff dough that is smooth and elastic (6 to 8 minutes total). Shape into a ball. Place in a lightly greased bowl. Turn once to grease surface. Cover and let rise in a warm place till double (about 1 hour).

● Punch dough down. Cover and let rest for 10 minutes. Divide into 12 portions. Shape each into an even circle, folding edges under. Press flat between hands. Place on 2 greased baking sheets. Press into 3-inch circles. Cover and let rise till nearly double (about 45 minutes).

   1 beaten egg white
   1 tablespoon water
      Caraway seed

● Combine egg white and water. Brush tops of buns with egg white and water mixture. Sprinkle with caraway seed. Bake in a 375° oven for 15 to 20 minutes. Remove from sheets. Cool on wire racks. Makes 12 buns.

Refrigerator Zucchini Pickles

3 cups thinly sliced firm zucchini
1 medium onion, quartered and thinly sliced
2 teaspoons salt

● Place zucchini and onion in a large glass or crockery bowl. Add enough lukewarm water to cover zucchini and onion, then stir in salt. Cover and let stand at room temperature for 2 hours. Drain off water, then rinse and drain thoroughly.

Pile 'em high on your favorite burger!

¾ cup vinegar
¾ cup sugar
½ teaspoon mustard seed
½ teaspoon celery seed
½ teaspoon ground turmeric

● In a medium saucepan combine vinegar, sugar, mustard seed, celery seed, and turmeric. Bring to boiling, stirring just till sugar is dissolved. Pour vinegar mixture over zucchini mixture. Cool to room temperature. Cover and chill for at least 24 hours before serving.

Store, tightly covered, in refrigerator for up to 1 month. Makes 3 cups.

Simple Barbecue Sauce

1 cup tomato juice
¼ cup packed brown sugar
¼ cup lemon juice
¼ cup catsup
2 tablespoons prepared mustard
2 tablespoons steak sauce
1 tablespoon paprika
1 teaspoon celery seed
¼ teaspoon pepper
Several dashes bottled hot pepper sauce

● In a small saucepan combine tomato juice, brown sugar, lemon juice, catsup, mustard, steak sauce, paprika, celery seed, pepper, and hot pepper sauce. Bring mixture to boiling. Reduce the heat and simmer, covered, for 15 minutes, stirring occasionally.

Brush sauce onto burgers often during the last 5 minutes of broiling or grilling.

Store, tightly covered, in refrigerator for up to 2 weeks. Makes about 2 cups.

Some people insist on barbecue sauce that's fiery hot; others yen for it sweet; and still others prefer it tart—but *everybody* likes it when it's as simple as this Simple Barbecue Sauce!

Crunchy Mustard

½	cup cold water	● In a medium mixing bowl stir together water, dry mustard, and mustard seed. Let mixture stand for 30 minutes.	**Whole mustard seed gives this spicy spread its unique crunch.**
½	cup dry mustard		
⅓	cup mustard seed		

⅔	cup dry white wine	● Meanwhile, in a medium saucepan combine wine, vinegar, brown sugar, onion, cinnamon, salt, turmeric, and allspice. Bring to boiling. Reduce the heat and simmer, uncovered, for 15 minutes. Strain the wine-vinegar mixture, discarding the solids.
½	cup vinegar	
¼	cup packed brown sugar	
2	tablespoons finely chopped onion	
¾	teaspoon ground cinnamon	
¼	teaspoon salt	
¼	teaspoon ground turmeric	
3	whole allspice	

| 1 | slightly beaten egg yolk | ● Stir egg yolk into mustard mixture. Stir *1 cup* of the hot wine-vinegar mixture into the mustard mixture. Return all to the saucepan. Cook and stir over medium heat till thickened and bubbly, then cook and stir for 2 minutes more. Remove from the heat and place saucepan in a bowl of ice water, stirring constantly for 1 to 2 minutes. |

Store, tightly covered, in the refrigerator for up to 2 months. Stir before serving. Makes about 1½ cups.

What's What in Prepared Mustards

Mustard is mustard—or so we used to think. Not so today, with dozens to choose from. To decide which one is for you, check this handy listing.
● *American mustard*—A sweet, tangy flavor and smooth texture characterize our yellow mustard.
● *French mustard*—Probably the most famous French mustard is Dijon. This grayish lemon-colored spread is made by combining ground mustard seeds with white wine, herbs, and spices.
● *German mustard*—The German mustard that's best known is Dusseldorf. It's dark colored and has a distinct aroma and a spicy sharp, yet sweet, flavor.
● *Chinese mustard*—This mustard packs a wallop. Its hot flavor comes from dark, pungent ground mustard seeds combined with water, vinegar, or even beer.
● *Flavored mustards*—You also can buy a variety of mustards that are flavored with everything from horseradish or jalapeño peppers to tomato puree.

Three-Fruit Chutney

2 cups cranberries
1 medium apple, peeled, cored, and chopped (about 1 cup)
¾ cup packed brown sugar
⅓ cup vinegar
¼ cup snipped dried apricots
⅛ teaspoon ground ginger
⅛ teaspoon ground allspice
⅛ teaspoon dry mustard

● In a 1½-quart saucepan combine cranberries, apple, brown sugar, vinegar, apricots, ginger, allspice, dry mustard, ¼ cup *water,* and ¼ teaspoon *salt.* Bring to boiling. Reduce the heat and boil gently, uncovered, for 18 minutes or till most of the excess liquid evaporates, stirring often. Cool to room temperature.
Store, tightly covered, in the refrigerator for up to 2 months. Makes about 2 cups.

Besides burgers, serve this chunky, tart chutney with sliced cooked ham, turkey, roast beef, or Indian curries.

Corn and Tomato Relish

1 cup fresh *or* frozen corn
¼ cup chopped onion
¼ cup vinegar
2 tablespoons sugar
2 tablespoons finely chopped celery
2 tablespoons finely chopped red *or* green sweet pepper
⅛ teaspoon mustard seed
⅛ teaspoon ground turmeric
1 medium tomato, peeled, seeded, and chopped (1 cup)

● In a 1½-quart saucepan combine corn, onion, vinegar, sugar, celery, sweet pepper, mustard seed, turmeric, 2 tablespoons *water,* and ¼ teaspoon *salt.* Bring mixture to boiling, stirring occasionally. Reduce the heat and simmer, uncovered, for 4 minutes. Remove from the heat and stir in chopped tomato. Cover and chill for several hours or overnight before serving.
Store, tightly covered, in the refrigerator for up to 5 days. Makes about 1½ cups.

Garden-fresh corn and tomatoes make this great summertime relish even better.

Garden Relish

½ cup white wine vinegar
4 teaspoons sugar
1 tablespoon olive *or* salad oil
½ teaspoon dried oregano, crushed
1 cup sliced cauliflower
1 stalk celery, thinly bias sliced (about ½ cup)
1 small carrot, chopped (about ⅓ cup)
½ of a medium green *or* red sweet pepper, chopped (about ¼ cup)

● In a bowl combine the vinegar, sugar, oil, oregano, ½ teaspoon *salt,* and ⅛ teaspoon *pepper;* set aside. In a 2-quart saucepan combine cauliflower, celery, carrot, sweet pepper, and ⅓ cup *water.* Bring mixture to boiling. Reduce the heat and simmer, covered, for 3 minutes. Remove from the heat and stir in the vinegar mixture. Cool to room temperature. Cover and chill for at least 24 hours before serving, stirring occasionally.
Store, tightly covered, in the refrigerator for several days, stirring occasionally. Makes about 2 cups.

Enjoy this crunchy, fresh-tasting relish anytime; the vegetables are available year-round.

Simple Barbecue Sauce
(see recipe, page 72)

Kraut Relish
(see recipe, page 77)

Corn and Tomato Relish

Cucumber Relish
(see recipe, page 77)

Crunchy Mustard
(see recipe, page 73)

Three-Fruit Chutney

Refrigerator Zucchini Pickles
(see recipe, page 72)

Garden Relish

Fines Herbes Mayonnaise

¼ teaspoon salt
¼ teaspoon dry mustard
⅛ teaspoon paprika
   Dash ground red pepper

1 egg yolk
1 tablespoon vinegar
1 cup salad oil
1 tablespoon lemon juice
½ teaspoon fines herbes,
   crushed

● In a small mixer bowl combine salt, mustard, paprika, and red pepper.

● Add egg yolk and vinegar. Beat with an electric mixer on medium speed till combined. Add oil, 1 teaspoon at a time, beating constantly. Continue beating in oil, 1 teaspoon at a time, till ¼ *cup* oil is added. While continuing to beat, add remaining oil in a thin, steady stream. Beat in lemon juice. Stir in fines herbes.

  Store, tightly covered, in refrigerator for up to 1 month. Makes 1¼ cups.

Make your own blend of fines herbes by stirring together 1 tablespoon dried *thyme,* 1 tablespoon dried *savory,* 1 tablespoon dried *marjoram,* 1 tablespoon dried *leaf sage,* and 1 tablespoon dried *basil.* Store the mixture in an airtight container. Crush the seasoning before using it. Makes about ¼ cup.

Kraut Relish

½ cup vinegar ⅓ cup sugar	● In a medium saucepan combine vinegar and sugar. Bring to boiling, stirring just till sugar is dissolved. Cool.	Jazz up Reuben sandwiches with some of this tart-sweet relish.
1 16-ounce can sauerkraut, drained ½ cup chopped celery ½ cup chopped green *or* red sweet pepper ¼ cup sliced green onion 1 2-ounce jar pimiento, drained and chopped	● Meanwhile, in a large mixing bowl combine sauerkraut, celery, sweet pepper, green onion, and pimiento. Stir vinegar-sugar mixture into sauerkraut mixture. Cover and chill for several hours or overnight before serving, stirring occasionally.	
	● Store, tightly covered, in refrigerator for up to 2 weeks. Makes about 3 cups.	

Cucumber Relish

1 medium cucumber, seeded	● Coarsely shred cucumber. Wrap in cheesecloth and press out excess liquid.	Double or even triple this no-fuss recipe and have relish for a crowd!
2 tablespoons finely chopped onion 2 tablespoons vinegar 1 tablespoon chopped pimiento ¼ teaspoon celery seed ⅛ teaspoon salt ⅛ teaspoon pepper	● In a small mixing bowl combine cucumber, onion, vinegar, pimiento, celery seed, salt, and pepper. Cover and chill for several hours or overnight.	
2 tablespoons mayonnaise *or* salad dressing	● Just before serving, drain cucumber mixture well. Stir in mayonnaise or salad dressing. Serve immediately. Makes about ⅔ cup.	

Homemade Horseradish Sauce

6 ounces fresh horseradish, peeled and coarsely chopped (1 cup) (see photo, below)
½ cup milk
¼ cup vinegar
2 tablespoons brown sugar
2 teaspoons Dijon-style mustard
½ teaspoon salt
⅛ teaspoon pepper

● Place chopped horseradish, milk, vinegar, brown sugar, mustard, salt, and pepper in a food processor bowl or blender container. Cover and process or blend till finely grated. The mixture will not be smooth (see photo, below).

In a small saucepan cook and stir horseradish mixture till heated through. *Do not boil.* Cool completely. You should have about 1⅓ cups.

Heating the grated horseradish mixture tones it down a bit. For a sauce with *lots* of bite, just forget this step.

¼ cup whipping cream

● In a small mixer bowl whip cream till soft peaks form. Fold in *¼ cup* horseradish mixture. Cover and chill for at least 1 hour before serving. Store, tightly covered, in the refrigerator for up to 2 weeks. Makes about ½ cup. **Note:** Store remaining horseradish mixture, tightly covered, in the freezer. Combine equal parts whipping cream, whipped, and thawed horseradish mixture, as needed.

Use a sharp knife to cut the brown, slightly knobby outer skin off the fresh horseradish root.

Process or blend the horseradish mixture till it's finely grated, but don't expect the mixture to be smooth.

Index